# Afghanistan Stories

# Praise for *Afghanistan Stories*

I want to tell you how exquisite your chapter on "The Party" was! One of the most beautiful chapters I ever read in any book.

This collection of sharp impression of living three years in Afghanistan, with irresistible titles, like 'Where Buddha Got His Clothes', 'Goat', 'Foreigners as Amusement', 'Books, Problems With Thinking, and the Gardens of Nimla' . . . by the gifted American author, William Barlak, is excellent!, an "Enchanting Read".

—Jim Ivory, Academy Award, Director
Merchant Ivory Productions

☙ ❧

The author writes from his experience working in Afghanistan many years ago, but his stories are really timeless. They unveil a hidden spiritual world with important lessons for us today. With a keen intuition, he knew whom to seek, and where to be for his extraordinary encounters. His book reveals Afghanistan to be a geode —an ordinary looking, even battered and rough stone, which conceals wondrous crystals within.

—Dr. Allan Chinen, Jungian Psychiatrist, Professor, Author,
*The Muses of Truth and Transformation, In the Ever After,* . . .

☙ ❧

I've known William Barlak now for over two and a half decades and have always admired and appreciated his ability to tell the truth even if the truth hurts his argument or he has to look at his core beliefs with a critical eye. This I found very inspiring since as an Afghan I was raised to never talk negatively about faith, family and culture. *Afghanistan Stories* takes us along into a journey into Afghan life seen from the eyes of not an American but someone with a soul and heart connection to the land and its people. The stories are written with the most beautiful descriptive, painterly language that the reader literally can taste the food, see all the colors he sees and even smell the scents that he has experienced throughout his journey into a place and time that could never be again. In his book, William describes an Afghanistan rarely experienced by westerners, before the wars, the destruction of cities and villages, and later with cities filled with refugees and returnees from neighboring countries, and the wider world which naturally has changed the way people interact with foreigners compared to a time and a place that was fairly unchanged and untouched by globalization and modernism.

—Matin Maulawizada, Makeup Artist, Co-founder
of Afghan Hands, Education/Employment for widows.

# Afghanistan Stories

## From Before the Wars

William V. Barlak

Tribar Books

Tribar Books
San Francisco, CA

ISBNs: Paperback: 979-8-218-85500-0, eBook: 979-8-218-85501-7

Library of Congress Catalog Number: 2025923357
First Printing: 2025

# Dedication

*This book is dedicated to the everyday people of Afghanistan who taught me so much.*

*Sometimes—and it was not just the look of hunger, but the deep look of a child's eyes searching in garbage for something to eat or to sell—showed more depth and wisdom than the eyes of the educated, prosperous, and comfortable of the world.*

# Contents

# Prologue

This book is a Collection of stories, of experiences, of events, that I had or that were told to me by reputable, trustworthy people.

I lived in Afghanistan in the 1970's. I worked in the U.S. Peace Corps (President Kennedy, 1961). One joins for 2 years but I stayed 3. I felt that it took me a whole year just to learn the basics of the culture.

The Peace Corps philosophy is to work with local in-country colleagues and offer what skills one could, and learn together. This furthers Peace.

We did not live like most N.G.O.s, we lived simply on limited budgets, rode bicycles, lived in simple non modern houses, outhouses, a well.

The Peace Corp assignments in Afghanistan had a tremendous range; teaching English to help Afghans communicate with the modern world in all fields, technical education, media communications, agriculture, architecture, engineering, distributing wheat to famine struck areas. Possibly the most romantic assignment was the women vaccinators who traveled on horseback to inoculate women and children in remote areas. They could inoculate women, who otherwise would be ignored.

There are always those who suggest that Peace Corps is a tool of imperialism and volunteers were spies. One can always sit in an armchair, and talk about such things. I always chuckle, because most of us were so busy working, learning, bridging the language and cultural divide, and frankly being sick with, giardia, amoeba, fevers, that we had no time or energy for such tasks.

Also we were explicitly instructed to avoid anything possibly political or we would be terminated as volunteers.

Like every job opportunity, it is what you make of it.

I am curious by nature I want to understand the "Why", and what is under the surface. I sought to travel throughout the country, to meet interesting people, to explore the history, the music, the art, the culture and customs of the country. At the end of 3 years I felt I had barely scratched the surface. My life there was very rich, but not easy. Sickness was close as was the peculiar loneliness of being in the vast spaces of central Asia. All so far from the world that I grew up in. My family's background , mostly Ukraine, Stories of Nazi Camps, Russian Camps, Siberia, did help me deal with this very different culture and grasp situations like not acknowledging Afghan friends on the street "because", and the story "Leave and never come back".

I worked there for 3 years and later visited when I worked in the area for 3 more years. I've kept in contact with friends who survived the wars and kept up with the heart breaking events.

I hope this book helps people understand that yes people do think differently, have different values and ways. But that the people of Afghanistan, like all people in the world, share a remarkable human system of innately knowing what is good and what is bad, what is right and what is wrong. So under all the news and stories and beliefs these people are the same as people in every country. They seek to live and understand life as you or I. And they hold that helping and loving others is what we do as Humans.

# The Country

When you want to understand a country, a person, a place, a building, you ask about what happened before. Yet in the case of Afghanistan the media and the writers will tell you about the sensational, of events, of wars, of historical records. But there is little about the people, how did they live, how do they live, what will be? What was there before the wars? It is hard to get the Big Picture of any country, to see the deeper levels of a place, to see what currents are below the surface that create the world that we see and experience. In a land such as this, with its many cultures and levels and complexities and romanticized history, it is much, much harder.

The poet Wallace Stevens wrote, "Snowman," in which he said one must be cold a long time in order to see the beauty of the snow. So, too, one must be in contact with the Afghan lands and peoples a long time to just begin to understand—and so then to realize one never will. One can only be open and try.

My time there was decades ago, young and male. As such I was not privileged to have much contact with the world of Afghan woman. Being young and enthusiastic also blocked my perceptions of many things that would have greatly troubled me had I been older, like the treatment of women, corruption, the unnecessary poverty. I stayed three years, and almost another four in the region, and have maintained contacts and stayed current with events. And like so many who have been touched by the transcendence of this mountainous land, my heart too has been broken many times by what has happened there. I believe this book will give you a sense of another side of this land. This is a book of various stories to be read now and then. They are varied as is the land. There is no order to the stories.

This is simply a telling of people, and events and places. The time begins before the wars. There is information here that will displease some and please others. But this is simply my retelling of what I experienced. Others may have different memories or views; this is only natural. I respect that. If these stories appear disjointed, this is to be expected as they are pieces of people's lives thrown together. The names have been changed to respectfully protect the privacy of the individuals written about. Some are alive; most have passed on, many of them killed during the fighting. In those days one could travel to most areas.

Hopefully you will learn a bit more of this place, and hopefully there will be a bit more understanding, and embracing. The place I lived in is gone. The wars and globalization have changed much.

Yet the basic culture and thoughts and mentality, the customs, food, and so many basics are not much changed.

Afghanistan is a land of mountains and many nationalities and cultures, 30 ethnic groups and 40 languages. It is an ancient crossroads, where the vast worlds of India, of Iran/Persia and of Central Asia meet, with layers of civilizations, Zoroastrian, Hindu, Buddhist, and now Islam . . . and ruins and astounding artifacts. There were ancient contacts with their neighbors. It was a major trading hub of the Silk Road. Ancient Iran/Persia shared much including language. India was always a constant partner, and the Kingdoms to the north were also active. Ancient China had trade and religious ties. Buddhism came to China through this area. It even controlled parts of the north at one time. Being the only source of Lapis lazuli there were ties with ancient Mesopotamia and Egypt and then all the West. Alexander the Great came and Greek kingdoms were established and Greek art mixed with Buddhism. The Romans had contact. The Jewish communities, in every city, were established 2,500 years ago. They were not visitors or wanderers. They were an ancient integral part of the society. Interestingly many Pashtoons claim that they are descendants of the 10 Lost Tribes of Israel. Then the Armenians and so many, many others. The presence of the various religions also has added to this rich complexity, Hindu, Zoroastrian, Jain, Buddhism, Hinayana and Mahayana, Manichaeism, Mithraism, Judaism, Nestorian Christian and other Christian Churches, Sikhism and others, and now Islam in its various forms. All these people came and mixed with the people there and this simulation and ensuing creativity enriched all and new ideas spread and even Buddha acquired his clothes here.

The land was always the borderlands of the neighboring empires, ancient Persia, ancient India, and Central Asian. Its modern form was established by Pashtuns from Kandahar in the 1700s. They attacked Iran, wrecked the capital, beautiful Isfahan, then conquered neighboring non-Pashtun Hindu Kush lands. This brought them into contact with British India. Soon both Britain and Russia realized that it would be wise to have a buffer between their respective expanding empires clearly seen in the narrow Wakhan panhandle. So they stopped their own expansions into the Hindu Kush area and recognized the Pashtun state. Since then all of its neighbors have constantly attempted to sway it to their own agendas. And the Afghans have always sought to play one against the other and to profit from the competition. Sometimes this game was brilliantly successful—they did maintain independence through the colonial era—but they were less successful in regards to the USSR. There were three wars with the British. They won the first Afghan-British War mostly because of absolutely incredible British arrogance and incompetency. The Second War brought collapse. The Third War ended when Kabul was lightly bombed by an airplane. The Afghans agreed not to stir up Muslim unrest in India during WWI, and the British agreed to leave Afghanistan alone. There is much said about the country being the victor over Empires, always able to defeat conquerors. But actually it was conquered many times but being resource poor, no great agricultural plains or precious minerals, it was much more useful as a border between Empires, be it Safavid Iran, Mogul India, Imperial Russia or the British Empire. Yes they can fight but the statistics from the Soviet Invasion are sobering, 15,000 Soviet dead, 1-2 million Afghans dead.

Today Pakistan, Iran, India, various Arab states, Russia, the Central Asian states, NATO, the USA, China, the Salafi movement (seeking to remake the entire Islamic world into their own image), and the Iranian Shiite movements are some of the major competitors. All of these have their supporters within the country. Money talks and in such a country it talks big! However, the Afghan people have also always fought to live in peace and independence.

Even after becoming Muslims following the Arab invasions, they promptly pushed the Arabs out, saying that they were Muslim but wanted to rule themselves.

Most are Sunni Muslims, some Shia, Ishmaeli and other Muslim groups. But the Sunni are not monolithic. They are often often also connected to various Sufi groups, or teachers. Some are Taliban but others have very different orientations. There were small groups of Sikhs, Hindus, and stories about unusual groups and etc. In these days the non-Muslim communities have been pushed out and the non-Sunni have been harassed. And the ruling Pashtoon half of the country is very tense with the Tajik, Uzbek, Turkoman, etc.

Yes, they are people like all others on this planet. But, it is often forgotten, especially in the halls of power and halls of learning that people really are different in the ways they arrange and prioritize their lives. The thinking and values are different. Too often people on one side of the world think they understand people on the other side and vice versa. They assume that others think as they do. They interpret other people's actions in the same way they interpret their own. They see others in terms of what they know and have experienced. Yet people's lives and experiences have been so different. Some cultures value the individual above all; others value the family, the group, above all. For a Westerner to say they "know" what an Afghan thinks and does and for an Afghan to say the reverse is pure ignorance and arrogance. Perhaps it would be better if people approached each other with warmth but with an attitude of "I don't know you, but I am open to learn."

Afghanistan is a place of amazing beauty. Huge mountains are divided by lush irrigated valleys, terraced and filled with walled orchards and channels of clear running water. One has the experience of going from barren desert land to fields of bright green and entering sculpted adobe villages where even the mud-and-straw wall surfaces act to mute sound and encourage peace. One walks through the aged wooden gates of a walled orchard into geometrically planted squared, lowered irrigated beds of flowers and vegetables beneath arching trees, and bright red rugs spread on the ground to welcome guests. Sitting on rugs and cushions drinking tea or eating right next to flowers and running water is a sensory delight. Such an experience is never forgotten. And add to this the hospitality and kindness and smiles of your hosts. They have an almost Japanese sense of enjoying the simple essence of things, like sitting on a rug next to cold flowing water, or on a slightly raised earth platform completely surrounded by flowers. Simplicity and elegance and nature and open hearts, these are some of the great treasures of this land—a far cry from the headlines of war and violence. Yet this reality exists with the other. Hopefully this work offers a taste of the beauty of this land and of these very human people.

# ☙ 1 ❧

# Some Terms and People

**M**any terms and names occur just once in these stories, but several are more prominent and deserve some introduction.

Term, *Agha* means "sir" in Iranian Persian, but in Afghan Dari—old Persian—it is more important; a person called by this name is one of some distinction.

Person, In the stories Agha was educated in British India, from a prominent family, and was a member of the Afghan government, and a scholar.

Person, Nur Agha was his Sufi name, (Agha means Sir/Lord, Nur means Light, or Lord of Light). His proper name was Sayed Mohammed al Darvish Gailani. He has passed away. The Gailani Family, descendants of the saint/mystic Abdul Qadir Gailani (Baghdad, d.1166) are hereditary rulers over the Qadiri Dervishes. Such families often have hereditary rule over a Sufi order. Hopefully someone in the family takes the role seriously and fulfills it by living as a Sufi; otherwise it becomes merely about power and money. Most nonMuslims believe Sufis are all good, open-minded people. In truth some Sufi orders are open and very tolerant, but others are very rigid and are fundamentalists. History is full of their role as fanatic jihadists. But even in the open groups all power is focused in one individual. This led to problems when these groups fought the Soviets: everything had to be decided by the one leading individual, and delegating power was difficult. Nur Agha belonged to an open Sufi family, the oldest. He was always very clear about who the rigid Sufi families were and he was very outspoken. In fact he was always clear about what was right and wrong; he encouraged people to speak the truth, and this caused friction with many.

Term, **Bacha** means boy or servant, or any male of lower rank, an underling; it can even have a sexual connotation. In refined speech, it is pronounced "bacheh," but in everyday speech it is "bacha," so that is the spelling I have used.

Afghanistan is not alone. As in many countries "loosing face" is upsetting. Even when you help someone, some will resent you because they "lost face" by being weak.

In all authoritarian countries one does not have power, so you blame others. And so people have little practice in reflection and taking responsibility. Some Afghans blame outsiders for the wars, but . . .

And many blame outsiders for the corruption, yet it is an old custom.

Ethnic tensions have risen. Pashtoons, 50%, be it king, president or Taliban demand to rule. The others speak of separation.

## ⁌ 2 ⁍

# In the Beginning

Words of warning came to me soon after I began to live in Afghanistan. I had met a member of Agha's family before, and now that I was "in country," I was invited to the home to meet him and the other impressive family members. I recall I was greeted with typical generous Afghan hospitality. The food was very delicious and a bit more varied and spicy than the usual dishes. The family had been forced long ago by the British to live in India, so they had added those tastes to the traditional ones. I recall being impressed. Most Afghans spoke more than one language, but here, to Hindi, Urdu, and other subcontinent languages were added proper English, German, and a few other languages. They were a very educated Pashtun family. Pashtuns vary from the most sophisticated to what we call the Taliban today. Unfortunately this division was supported by the tribal systems.

After the meal it was time for tea (black in the evening) and more serious talk. They asked about my life, and vice versa, and then suddenly Agha asked, "What books have you read on Afghanistan?" I suddenly felt as if I were being grilled by a stern college professor. Fortunately I had read every book I could find about the area, and he said, "Good." Then he asked if I had read a particular book, and I said I had not heard of it. He handed me a copy (obviously he had prepared for this), told me to read it and to come back for dinner and tell him what I had thought of the book. I happily agreed and remember looking forward to the read. Well, as things usually are there, it was not so simple. I read the book and dutifully went back on the appointed day for another wonderful dinner and my book report, but I was very embarrassed at the same time. After dinner we all sat for tea and he asked me what I thought of the writer and the book. I said I didn't know what to say except that I was embarrassed and felt I should apologize for the author.

The man who wrote it was an American engineer who had come to the country in the first quarter of the twentieth century to set up some of the first electrical systems: dams, generators, and so on. He lived there for over a decade. The book was his memoir, published years ago when people were sometimes very "politically incorrect" and not so sensitive to others, but they were honest in their feelings. He said terrible things, such as Afghans stopped thinking at the age of twelve, and they did this and they did that. Agha was amused by my discomfort but kept asking for details of what was written, and I kept adding that it was years ago and that the man was obviously prejudiced.

Then Agha asked me if I thought the writer liked the Afghans. I said, "No, he hated you people and was very blunt and negative in what he said."

Agha then said, "No, you are wrong!" The other people in the room started commenting, and I recall feeling out on a limb, all alone and confused.

I said, "I don't understand what you just said. The book is very clear."

Agha said, "Yes, he hated us and laughed at us and said harsh things, but he lived here for some twelve years! A person of his education, income, and standing didn't need to do that. He laughed at us, but he also loved us, otherwise he would not have lived here and worked so hard to develop our resources for so long. You should remember that what one sees is not necessarily the reality in a country like this." Agha said he had given me that book to read for a reason, to teach me a lesson. He said, "When you think you understand us, you are wrong!"

He then related a story about how as a young man he had been assigned to help some anthropologists do research with some tribes. He went into details and explained how careful everyone was. Then he said he had read most of the histories and anthropological studies done on his people. "The engineer," he said, "understood us this much," and he stretched his thumb and index finger apart. He used his fingers to demonstrate a small amount. "The professors and anthropologists with all their training understand us this much," he said, and he moved his finger and thumb together until they were almost touching. He kept them there and stared at me.

Everyone in the room added their approval to his statement, and I felt relieved that the story was over and that I finally understood what all this was about, and it seemed very reasonable.

I tried to remember this lesson, and it really allowed me to be much more open to what was happening and, I believe, also much more open to possibilities. So many of the people I met would have been impossible to meet without this openness, and situations would have been impossible to arrange—meeting Nur Agha, the neighbor with the unexpected antelope, the prayer rug, the connections to the Land of Light, so many.

## ⧾ 3 ⧽

# Ziarat Boy

As you traveled anywhere in the country, you passed special graves, marked with piles of stones, and poles with flag-like pieces of cloth tied to them to symbolize prayers and vows. They were ziarats, shrines, sometimes humble, but sometimes grand structures were built. The bright blue shrine in Mazar-e Sharif was the largest. Many were domed buildings, often just a cube with an arch in each wall and a dome on top. This form was originally Zoroastrian, used in buildings that protected their sacred fires. Forms are adapted, as everywhere, from the preceding culture. And Islamic rulers were quick to use the best from their new subjects. The famous Dome of the Rock in Jerusalem, for example, is an octagonal dome form developed and used in Imperial Rome and Byzantium. And the interior mosaics, with calligraphy stating Islamic beliefs' ascendancy over Jewish and Christian beliefs, are the best work of artist from their archenemy—the Byzantine Empire. No expense was spared. In this part of the world the Byzantines are called Romans because they literally were. Even the poet Rumi is called "The Roman—Rumi" because he lived close to the border.

But here in the high mountains, the shrines were what people could do: rocks and a pole. Sometimes beautiful ancient trees surrounded a ziarat—proof that without irrigation, trees could grow there and thrive. It was clearly too many goats and sheep and lack of thought that had stripped their land of green. On roads like the Salang Road, the road through the Hindu Kush Mountains in the north of the country, there were markers and there were stories.

One such marker was to a young boy. Buses were sometimes truck chassis with makeshift bus shells added on, accommodating many jammed in, with their goods on top; they had drivers and helpers along with bachas, boys, who hung on the back or side and did necessary basic tasks.

There were poor children everywhere, then and now. Muslims can not adopt, (they can sponsor) so orphans or the homeless or children with parents too poor to care for them are sent to work. Girls are often sent to wealthier houses as servants, but due to their low status and lack of protection, they face being victimized by males of the household, and this leads to more problems and more uncared-for children. Boys are hired out as servants, errand boys, and can also be abused. The little ones are often collectors of reusable garbage, food, paper, plastics, anything that can be sold.

This kind of bacha, and usually another one or two worked for the driver. They would do whatever he ordered, whether they wanted to or not. They clearly knew that without education they were lucky to have any job at all. They fetched tea, or food, shopped, washed the bus, obeyed. The word *bacha*—a boy, a servant—has connotations of everything from lowly work or to being an inferior, to serving someone sexually.

Often they were zealous, full of energy. They were always thin and their clothes ragged, and even in the cold they had little to protect them, maybe a cap or coat. True, they were used to these temperatures, but cold is cold, and body heat does leave. Their eyes were big and they looked as if they were somewhat amazed all the time. Hunger does this, an almost cruel beauty. But, too, they were constantly trying to be aware of what was needed, of what all these big adults were doing; they needed to be alert to keep this job. But hunger saps energy and focus. So they tried harder; after all they were desperate.

This group—the driver, a helper or two —kept the show on the road. And they were a family of sorts. If they cooperated all might be well, might be better. The trip could be made, the bus, the truck, might hold together for another trip, life could go on.

Of course there was the great adventure—in a land where people largely stayed with their family circles, this group was surrounded by all sorts of strangers, passengers. They saw people from different areas, different clothes, faces, skin colors, languages. They even saw people from other countries. And they saw the countryside and they saw different cities and towns. For a youngster this is a great wonder.

But since each seat had a price and the aisles and roofs were usually loaded with possessions, there was no room for the bachas. They sat on top, on top of baggage, or stood on the back bumper holding on to metal rings or ladders to the roof. These kids hung on for dear life; they held on for hours. There was no choice. When it was cold it was harder.

Some vehicles, old or horrifically overloaded, had a hard time on slopes, so when it slowed and began to stop, a boy, a bacha, would jump off and wedge a large block of wood behind the wheels to keep it from rolling back. When the engine was revved up sufficiently to continue the climb, the bachas would pull up the block and race to get back on the moving vehicle.

In this story, the bus was stalling on the Salang Road, the main road to the north, which climbs and climbs on switchbacks until it tunnels through the Hindu Kush Mountains at 11,200 feet. It started to roll back; people were screaming, "Back!" It was a twisty road with dramatic drops and no guardrails. The boy jumped off and tried to position the blocks, but it was not working: there was too much momentum. It kept moving backwards—nothing to stop the bus—a turn in the road and a cliff was near. He threw himself under the wheel and stopped the sliding. The riders were saved. Some say he accidently slipped under the wheel; who knows. Either way the people were saved.

A large pile of stones and several poles with flags marked his grave. I always saw passengers pray when they passed it. Actually, we all prayed.

## ☙ 4 ❧

# The Ocean and
# Mr. Potato

This is a classic Afghan story. It is the story of Mr. Kachaloo, in English Mr. Potato.

We have to go back to the late 1940s, when the British were withdrawing from the subcontinent. At that time, the Afghan government re-declared its support for Pashtunistan. Pashtunistan technically is all the land inhabited by the Pashtun, or Pakhtun, people. This includes southern and eastern Afghanistan, the North-West Frontier Province of Pakistan, and some say Baluchistan, or basically all of Pakistan west of the Indus River. A huge area

In 1893, the Durand Line was drawn by the British to separate their empire from the Afghans. Nowadays it forms the technical border between Pakistan and Afghanistan. It was imposed on the Afghans and cut right through the middle of Pashtun tribal lands.

Families and tribes were split by this line. But since the tribal areas were ungovernable by outside forces and the tribal councils ruled themselves, it was not such a tragic event or as severe as it could have been. Arbitrary political decisions such as this one, made in the Victorian drawing rooms of London, normally would have produced great human suffering. But this was Central Asia. The line cuts through the heart of the real tribal areas. Here no outside government has ever ruled with any authority. The land is very mountainous and harsh, poor, and the people have been raised amidst blood feuds, vendettas, for thousands of years. And for ages anyone wishing safe passage to or from India for business, war, plunder, or what have you would have to bribe their way through the mountain passes, the most famous being the Khyber Pass, or face attack or worse—endless harassment and skirmishes, guerrilla war from guerrilla war experts. This is the heartland for the Taliban and was for al-Qaeda.

Thus being "warlike" was and is a livelihood, a profession. War here is not something unusual; small-scale war in these areas is simply normal. This is a fact that most outsiders never seem to comprehend; it goes against their idea of basic reality. Of course there are drawbacks, like lack of "development." These areas just have not developed in the usual ways. Sometimes the settlements look like a frontier area, everything looks like it was built not that long ago, when in actuality things have always looked that way. They simply have not built in more permanent-looking ways, or there is little infrastructure—good roads can bring the government or one's enemies quicker.

Sometimes the area looks to be poor, the people simply dressed; yet they may actually be well off. In some areas it is considered bad taste to live much better than one's fellow tribesmen, sort of like some of the "old money" in Swiss cities and other places. I knew of very wealthy, powerful families who dressed and acted almost the same as their tenant farmers. The tribes just kept ruling themselves and still do, playing government and enemy tribes off against each other. It is like a continual chess game to them. These days peoples from the Middle East and Westerners have entered this game. Of course this is all a man's world, a tribal world. The women are kept inside the large high walled adobe Qalas, forts. They have no free movement. Some rarely are allowed out. Women it must be remembered are a sign of tribal "honor" and are paid for in dowries and thus a kind of property. Some of these tribal customs violate Islamic law.

But the Durand Line was and is contested. Pashtuns sometimes advocate their own state, Pashtunistan—eastern and southern Afghanistan along with most of Pakistan west of the Indus River. The Afghan government, claims all this land across the border, including Karachi, as part of Afghanistan. Of course the people in Pakistan have had a different history, their land is more developed and they have contributed much to modern Pakistan. Do they wish to be joined to Afghanistan is a question only they can decide. Interestingly Pakistan is currently building a wall along the Durand line to separate and control.

Of course, Pakistan could also claim part of Afghanistan. This parallels the situation in Kashmir today: India claims it, Pakistan claims it, and most Kashmiris just want to be left alone and have their own state.

Now at one time, the Afghan authorities decided that having a seacoast was inevitable and decided to prepare for it. A naval department was established, complete with budget. People would point out its building—a small structure all alone at the base of a barren mountain near the Intercontinental Hotel, then on the outskirts of town.

It was forlorn-looking, empty, engulfed in brown space in front and all around, and hundreds of miles from the Indian Ocean. The government also sent a bright young man overseas to get the best education in marine sciences. This was a smart move since very, very few people, if anyone, in the country had familiarity with the field. In fact, most people had never even seen a sea, or any large body of water.

In fact, it was hard for the people to conceive of such a thing—so much water! They simply did not have any experience or exposure to it, just as most people reading this have no idea how to weave a rug or irrigate a patch of desert, skills or concepts second nature to an Afghan. Once when I was teaching women airline stewards we were discussing geography and oceans. One of the brightest students asked me if an ocean was as wide as the Kabul river in spring flood? I was shocked into their reality. The river is small and dries up in summer.

The young man was a good student and spent his years abroad learning as much as he could about this area, but also about science and health matters in general. After years of study, he returned eager to help his country in their new endeavor. Unfortunately, the government's political ideas and South Asian political reality did not mesh. Every year the government would push for Pakistan to give back what they felt was rightfully their land. And every year Pakistan, not wishing to divest itself of half of its territory, would refuse, and troubles resulted. There were border closures, rumors of possible war, of revolts of this tribe and that, of coming secret changes and always the threat that the Pashtun people would rise up in a massive movement and then . . . ! When information is not available, rumors fly.

This "yes but no" situation was very hard on the scientist. Here he was, trained, eager to advise and help the government, but his budget and importance fluctuated with the political situation.

He would walk the streets frustrated and full of information that could help his people. He saw many things that he knew from his scientific training to be unhealthy and harmful. For instance, in the wealthier areas of town, people would throw out peelings and bones and such outside their compound walls. This would be eaten by the stray dogs and other animals; sometimes the wolves came. But usually the children of the very poor would have a bag or a large tin can strapped to their back and all day long they would collect items that they could sell—recycling bones, various metals, and plastic bags. Peelings, such as potato peelings, could be fed to animals or chickens, or unfortunately some children were so hungry that they would eat these leftovers themselves. They filled their stomachs and they felt better for a while.

Now, the young man would see this and, knowing the terrible health hazards of eating garbage, would get upset. He would yell at the kids not to do this: "It's dangerous! Don't eat the potatoes!" They, on the other hand, poor and always hungry, would think him absolutely crazy. If we don't eat this, what do we have?—empty stomachs, dizziness and the gnawing, haunting pain of hunger. He was stupid, not logical at all. They had heard that he had been educated abroad. Also, at times *horagis*, foreigners, urged them to do as he said, "Don't eat it." These were not logical or practical people, the children obviously decided. So when he started to yell, they put the word "Mr.," which everyone knew signified someone from "outside" and added it to their word for potato—*kachaloo*. When they saw him coming, and, anticipating what he would say, they would yell out, "Mr. Kachaloo, Mr. Kachaloo." And because they felt his craziness was associated with living abroad, they began to call all foreigners Mr. Potato, even women.

So you would walk down a street and these little street kids would yell out "Mr. Kachaloo." You could get hostile or you could enjoy the title. If you responded hastily and yelled at them, they might throw stones at you and run. But if you joked with them and laughed, these little kids—so hungry, dressed in ragged clothes, with dirty hands and faces, with big silver tin cans almost as big as they were tied to their backs, full of pieces of bones and such— would laugh with you.

# ❧ 5 ❧

# Where Buddha Got His Clothes

T he prince Siddhartha Gautama, known as Buddha, was born in what is now Nepal and also lived in India. His teachings, the Dharma, spread throughout the subcontinent and came to the mountains of Afghanistan. In the early days the emphasis was on the ideas, the concepts. There were no images: symbols, yes, statues and portraits, no. The movement was a reform, and as the Hindus will say, it was a reform movement within the Hindu world. Of course the Buddhists see it as a separate structure. In those early days the Buddha was represented by symbols: a *stupa* (a mound-like structure), a lotus flower, and others.

But here in the northwest corner of the Indian subcontinent, in these mountains, there were vigorous cultures that had developed. They were a mixture of the various local ones and the remnants of the great empire of Alexander the Great. "Skandar" is still an important figure in the minds of people in this area even today, a testament to his accomplishments. Classical Greek civilization was set up everywhere and then mixed with the local. There were Greek cities, columns, art, coins, plays performed in outdoor theaters, literature, and statues.

When Buddhist missionaries came here, they met this bubbling cultural scene. So here the symbols from the subcontinent met the vigorous image makers and here they began to carve statues of Buddha. Here he acquired a classical body and the beautiful draped clothing of the Greek world. To this was added certain characteristics from his home, such as the curled hair and the knot of hair on top of his head. He was now a three-dimensional image, and soon the story of his life was also put into stone and clay. These images and whole dioramas of scenes from his life were used as teaching tools. This explosion of form is known by the name of a kingdom: Gandhara. It became a great center of Buddhist education; the two major schools, Hinayana and Mahayana, were present. And missionaries went forth into Central Asia and on to China, Korea, and Japan. And that is why those Japanese statues so far, far away, have the graceful folds of classical Greek drapery on the body of the Buddha. These mixed people took to the new faith enthusiastically. Huge monasteries and stupas were built. The stupa near Peshawar, Pakistan, was hundreds of feet high.

Some places, such as Hadda, were of the Hinayana school. Bamiyan had one 280-foot statue, another of 240 feet, and smaller ones, carved, plastered, and painted into the cliffs of the Hindu Kush. These represented the Mahayana school, with Buddha as the Lord of the Universe. Here hundreds of monks lived and studied in cave rooms carved into these cliffs. Each room had a view overlooking the farms and fields of the valley and the snow-capped mountains, truly a place to be reflective. Even now Afghan Buddhist libraries are found with manuscripts on birch bark. Today there are no forests, no such trees within sight. This is another testimony to the environmental degradation. Here too technology was expanded; it now is reported that the first oil paints in the world were developed here to decorate these cave shrines. Some of the caves are worked so that the ceilings resemble intricately carved wood ceilings.

It was a place of learning as well as of spirituality. And as if to reinforce the spiritual meaning of Banyan, just a bit west lie the surreal turquoise lakes of Band-e Amir, whose dam like walls are formed by the minerals from its own waters.

Here in this mountain valley pilgrims came from as far away as China. These Chinese scholars reported that people entered the valley bowed, and did not look up. Later in the evening they would assemble in front of a colossal statue. Music and chanting began, horns blared, and as people looked up in awe, fire embers were poured down from openings near the head, and the gold- and gem-covered face glowed as the Lord of the Universe became manifest for them. And they were also taught that all was *maya*, illusion.

When the Arab Muslim armies attacked, the people bowed and became members of the new faith, but as soon as the armies withdrew, they went back to their old ways. Reports say they went back and forth eight or nine times until, faced with the ultimatum of genocide, they submitted. This whole part of the world has these underlying levels of civilization—the early cultures, then Zoroastrian, Buddhist, and Islamic. Even the name of Bukhara, a city in Uzbekistan, famous in Islam, comes from the Indian Sanskrit word *vihara*, monastery.

Rumi's family were said to be Buddhist scholars. All this points to the fact that the famous Silk Road was about much more than the transport of silk. Here Hindus, Zoroastrians, Buddhists, numerous Nestorian Christians, Muslims, and all the others met and exchanged goods, ideas, concepts, technologies, and culture.

Eventually wars and invasions brought ruin. Interestingly the huge carved Bamiyan Buddhas had smooth face surfaces not faces with features, thus lending credence to stories that the faces were originally gold-covered wood that were taken down and hidden. The Mughals of India used the statues for cannon target practice, and for years men used the statues and paintings of the *kuffar*, unbelievers, for rifle practice, because faces are haram, forbidden. The statues survived, beloved by the local Shiite Hazara people, until the Taliban, financed by the Gulf States, Saudi Arabia, and Pakistan, poured into the country and into the valley in their new Japanese pick-up trucks. It took real effort to destroy them. Chechen engineers, fierce from their battles with Russia, did the job. Hated local Shiite Hazara men, lowered by ropes, were used by the Pashtun Taliban to plant the explosives. Across the country thousands of statues and sites and museums were destroyed; others were sold to Pakistani dealers.

A very educated Afghan gentleman once told me that even he, who was aware of the country's glorious history, had been indifferent to it. He said this was due to the educational system that, then as now, mentioned these past glories but stressed that only when the Arabs came with their faith did civilization really begin. He said that the world's interest in his country helped open his eyes wider, and he said the more he learned about his country's past the more he wanted to learn, and the more he was amazed.

Once Daud, an archeologist, took a group of us to see a great stupa outside Ghazni. There were said to be some two thousand stupas in the country, mostly unexcavated, but now probably pillaged. At this location there were levels of building, one over the other: Hindu, Buddhist, and others, several burnt, thus preserving some. Here were the feet of a colossal figure; it was still colored. The bases of other figures could be seen, as well as wonderfully intricate decorations. The realistic feet and legs and small figures were shocking in their naturalness. From the ground up to about a meter high, there was a realistically portrayed world, and then above this line was nothing—just destroyed, empty space and views of the stark, brown treeless desert with its natural trees and grasses also lying in destruction.

It took great skill and talent to fashion these figures and all the other thousands across the land. The archeologist pointed out another ruined stupa to the east. He said a line of them stretched east all the way to India. And from where we stood on that hill, there was no one who could create such realistic beauty in that area or perhaps in the whole country.

In Fondukistan, a poor, remote area to the northwest of Kabul, statues were found in walled-up rooms. Here there had been a small Buddhist monastery and here were statues; some say they represent the highest flowering of the mix of Indian and Greek sculpture schools. One group was of a man and a woman seated half facing each other, half facing you, in mere clay. But they were decorated with regal clothing and jewels, with faces that expressed grace and culture. And the very elegant, unnatural, long fingers from outstretched open hands are of a greatly sophisticated style. Half the statues were sent to the Kabul Museum with unfortunate results. The other half are safe in Paris at the Musée Guimet.

A Bodhisattva, Fondukistan, near Bamyan, 700 C.E., from the last days of Buddhist Art before Islam. A brilliant blending of Greco-Roman, Indian (Gupta), and Sasanian (Iran) art.

They have lost so much, but much is still there and much has been recorded, and there are always new discoveries. Recently very early Buddhist scriptures written on birch bark have been discovered, proving that there were extensive forests then and that here were centers of sophisticated learning. With increased awareness of all the great and varied strings of their rich and diverse past, the peoples of Afghanistan can someday play wonderful, wonderful music for the world. How many countries hold such varied histories and cultures and arts?

## ᗏ 6 ᗍ

# He, the Rug, and I

andshakes, as in all cultures, could convey many differing messages. Men and women usually didn't shake hands, though the urban ones did. Conservative men wouldn't ever shake a foreign woman's hand. Women would shake hands with women. But of course it was all done with greater intimacy and warmth. Kissing on the cheeks was commonplace, but only women with women, men with men; sometimes once, or twice, or more. Some tribal groups would move as if to kiss but would quickly stop short, once, twice, three times. If a man shook another man's hand and extended his index finger so that its tip pressed against the palm of his hand, this meant that he wanted to have sex with him.

Women shook hands with women, men shook hands with men, all the time, in greetings, in farewells, to co-workers every morning, it took time. A "Salaam Aleykum," a handshake, then right hand over heart, a ritual chant begins—"*How are you? Are you well? Your health? Your family? Your _____? Your _____?" On and on, it is intoned at the other person, interspersed with ritual thank yous, all simultaneously.

For very high-ranking people the hand of the senior was kissed or held and bowed to or brought to one's forehead. Some groups only gingerly shook fingers. Other people shook heartily. Some became quite animated holding on to each other. Sometimes hands were not withdrawn but held as people conversed, to press a point, to show warmth. It was fun to watch Americans, or Westerners, or other Asians, who are not used to much or any same-sex physical contact, have their first "long handshake." You could sense their embarrassment and discomfort as the conversation went on and on and yet they were still holding hands! Some adapted, others never did, and a few went into the feeling and enjoyed the intimacy as the Afghans did.

On my first trip north, across the Hindu Kush mountains, I stayed in Kunduz, a modern town founded in drained malarial swamps—new irrigation works allowed cotton to be grown, new wealth! Pashtuns were brought in to settle and reap profits. Neighboring Tajiks and Uzbeks watched.

On the wall in a small rug store there was a deep rust–mahogany brown rug with diamond-shaped medallions in rows. I later learned this design is called a Kunduz Yomud, a Turkoman. It was a standard four feet by seven feet with only one edge patch. Its deep, almost metallic color—it had tremendous bark, sheen—attracted me, and unfortunately I showed my reaction. And I began to bargain. It was my first time and I was lucky that the dealer sensed this and was out for a good time.

He quoted ridiculous sums to me. I said I loved it, so he laughingly raised the price. We argued, then I threatened to walk out with it. He then grabbed my hand as if to shake it but didn't let go. I pulled back. He pulled. I felt as if I was falling through levels of emotion after emotion, anger, humor, fear. Beyond embarrassment, and now more desperately wanting the rug, I surrendered to his holding my hand and began to feel that we were brothers united by the rug, both people, now connected physically, if only for a while, both of us inhabiting a shared space. There was just the two of us. Sure, others were watching amidst their own conversations. But we were in our own world, he, the rug, and I.

We enjoyed our drama; I was told it lasted two hours. I had no recollection of time. In the end we agreed on a price. We shook hands with the money between our palms, my right hand in his with the money between our palms. This was often done to seal a good, clean deal and to sincerely wish the other well. The rolled rug under my left arm, smiles on both our faces, we wished each other well and I walked home with my treasure.

The rug, one of my very favorites, was stolen many years later. I miss it, but I do have the memory of "the buying," and "my brother" who taught me to enjoy, to let go, to try to be "in the moment."

# The Lady Told the King

One day a student said she had an important story to tell—something had just happened and she was all excited by it. Anywhere in the world where there are limitations to free speech, rumors and stories become very, very important.

At that time, there was a drought in most of the country and a famine in parts. There were many conflicting stories about what was real or not. We had heard rumors of it and had also been cautioned by authorities not to discuss or explore the subject, or we might be asked to leave the country.

In true Afghan fashion, the stories ranged from one extreme to the other, from whole areas being depopulated to "oh, it's just drier than usual." One story said that the king did not know of it. He was kept ignorant of it by his family and his advisors.

One day an elderly, grand lady, from an important family, a Mohammadzai, the royal clan, well respected by all, decided "enough of these rumors of famine and denials." She decided to see for herself. She first went south to the Kandahar area, traveled around, and asked questions, incognito, just as a person, not as someone serving in some government capacity, and not as a person of her rank and status. She did not use her family name.

Then she moved westward exploring the situations, the needs, and the government response, in each district until she got to the city of Herat. There she came across large numbers of refugees from the eastern mountains and from the north, who were selling off their possessions for food. Many were destitute, and the governor was doing little to help. Some people were going to these families and selecting some of the children. They made arrangements that in exchange for food and money, the children—boys and girls—would be taken to "good homes to work as servants." Of course it was more than this, as everyone knew. Yes, some were saved and did work as servants legitimately, but others were treated badly and worse. People were bought. Since they had no family to protect them, they were easy targets of abuse.

Stories were told that later, during the Soviet onslaught and then during the civil war, children were captured by various factions and the attractive ones sold off. Many ended up in Pakistan; others, especially children of parents who supported the various Soviet-led governments, were taken or sold to fundamentalist groups who sold them off to Saudi Arabian or Gulf State families where they were never heard from again. The boys and girls, so-called servants, obviously were said to be used for sex as well.

Well, this lady became more and more alarmed and enraged at the horrible situation and the poor government response to it. She returned to Kabul, called the palace and announced that she was coming, period! Being a woman, especially older, from an important family, she had more clout than most. She demanded to see the king immediately. Not taking no for an answer, she pushed and fumed until she had her way and got in. Then she commenced to tell him in detail of what she had seen and to furiously denounce him and berate him for his inaction in the face of such massive suffering.

The story goes that he was deeply shocked by this news. He was not upset by her verbal attacks at all; in fact he felt them justified. He thanked her profusely and vowed that he would not eat, he would fast, until relief supplies relieved the hunger of his people. When they ate, he would eat, he vowed.

The person who told me this story knew the lady of the story and, when questioned, said she believed it totally. The rest of the group who listened to the story had nodded and made appropriate remarks during the story's telling. These were often one-syllable expressions:

- *woh woh*—oh, oh; or good
- *bah*—great, good
- a click of the tongue—too bad.

They seemed very involved in the story and deeply touched.

When it was over, I asked them if they believed the lady. Yes, they went along with the storyteller, they believed the lady went and did what was said she did. I then asked if they believed the king's response and his being unaware of the extent of the disaster. Their eyes turned cold in an instant—"No, it's a lie, a show. He knew." They all agreed.

## ᚦ 8 ᚦ

# A Walk in Nuristan

*tan* means "country" or "land of"; *nur* means "light." Nuristan means the land of light. This refers to its conversion by jihad, holy war, to Islam in the 1890s by the ruthless King Abdul Rahman. It was convert or be killed. It is also known as Kafiristan, land of unbelievers. Kipling wrote of it in "The Man Who Would Be King." Some of the kafirs refused to convert and crossed the Durand Line into British-controlled territory, now Pakistan. They are called Kalash and maintain their unique religion, polyphonic singing, and customs amid great pressure to convert. This area, heavily forested, high and very remote, drew people and people's fantasies.

Mentioned at the time of Alexander the Great, they claimed common ancestry since they had ivy and had a god of wine. There were many stories and legends about them—that they were descendants of the Greeks, or a product of intermarriage, or were much older. Their light coloring and light hair and eyes—even red or blond hair and blue eyes—were legendary, as was their former prowess in war and their brightness and clarity of thought.

Once on a bus in Kabul I noticed a man staring at me. I looked back and he then asked what country I came from. After explaining,

I asked him what part of Nuristan he was from. He laughed and said,

"How did you know I was from Nuristan?" I answered, "Because you have big eyes." He liked this directness, we chatted. His name was Azziz, was from a side valley up the Darya Pech, the River Pech, and he invited me to visit. I said I would try; I was thrilled. I asked him if I would use horses to get there. He said, "Not unless you are strong enough to carry them! Mountains!"

Getting there was not so easy. Most tourists went up north of Jalalabad along the Kunar River to Assadabad. There was a government checkpoint there. They then continued north along the river to the villages of Mandigal and Kamdesh. They went there, so, naturally, I wanted to go any other place possible. Azziz's town was west of Assadabad along the Darya Pech then north up a river valley. It took time to get informed. I needed permission from the government interior ministry. Azziz was a local khan, or leader, so his sponsorship would help, and I did have his verbal invitation. Later it turned out that the family of a man I tutored was influential in the area; he offered his family's generous help—most of all by offering their name, a jeep and driver, and another son to accompany us. It turned out that they were related to Azziz, and in fact much later I learned that Azziz was returning from a visit to their home in Kabul when I had met him on the bus. A true case of synchronicity—the odds of this happening! But in Afghan fashion, it was meant to happen. Many things happened there in this way.

I then went to the government ministry with a letter identifying myself and stating an itinerary. The ministry was in an imposing edifice with polished marble halls and a garden donated by the Japanese government that ingeniously incorporated Japanese and Afghan garden features in a dry landscape. The building was severe, and the people inside self-important and tense, suspicious of any possible espionage. But amidst the marble an old quilt hanging over a doorway marked where a bacha, a servant, made tea, and ran errands from. It was through their help that connections were made. I went to the Baba with a gift and soon I had my letter of permission.

In the course of investigation I had learned that very few people entered this side of Nuristan. Some years no one entered, other years only a few. I was told that the year before, two Frenchmen had gone in. There was some problem, and one or both of them were shot dead at a teahouse. As there basically were no teahouses in Nuristan, it must have been in the Pashtun areas that surrounded it to the east and south. I knew that besides the Afghan friends it would be prudent to have some other foreigners along—less chance of disappearing. So I invited M. and D.

On the appointed morning Abdul, son of the khan Azziz, adventurous and helpful, arrived with his driver, Mystery. In the eastern areas mechanics were given this nickname—there must be a story behind this from the days of British India. I was told the name came into use from the way people could fix cars and machines so ingeniously—it was a mystery. We packed up, stopped at the ministry, more paperwork, and headed for Jalalabad east on the highway through the dangerous, narrow and very deep Tangi Garu gorge. We went north from Jalalabad up a very broad valley that narrowed. The huge snow-topped mountains of Nuristan loomed to the northwest and north. To the northeast was mountainous Pakistan, Dir and Bajaur, Pashtun tribal areas, and Chitral, and beyond them the roof of the world, the Karakorums and Himalayas.

East of Kabul was all Pashtun area. We passed through the village of Shewaki, where wooden bowls were lacquered in red and dark colors. Sugar bowls and lids looked like miniature stupas with eight-spoked wheel designs on the side—like the Buddhist Wheel of Life.

The gravel road soon paralleled the broad, swift Kunar River. The river was silvery, gleaming metallic in the sunlight. It felt like we were entering a different world. Later when I went up to it, I found that it was due to small flakes of mica in the water. It was not an inviting river. It felt deep and treacherous.

It was summer, so Kabul was hot, but downhill in Jalalabad and Kunar, it was really hot. Only as we approached Nuristan did it again cool. We passed cemeteries; some graves were marked by carved rectangular-like structures with pointed roofs like little Western houses—there were no houses built this way in the country. They were about a meter high, and projecting out from both pointed roof ends were boards cut into what could be interpreted as abstract horses' heads.

Assadabad was an energetic town. Almost any town in the east near the tribal areas, even if it had been there for centuries, felt like a frontier town—these places had town features but were unfinished or just started and they also had that clear feeling of being on the edge of something, where something established ended and an area of uncertainty, of unknowingness, began. Lots of men with guns.

The setting was gorgeous—two roaring rivers, soaring mountains, but the town was not beautiful. Yet it was an energetic market town, full of Sikh shops. Yes, in the midst of very conservative Islamic tribesmen, there were many Sikhs and Hindus—they lived together well. Here you saw tall, heavy, armed men, with bullet belts across their chests walking hand in hand with their "friends." Few women were visible. We went to the compound of relatives outside of town alongside the river. We drove up to high mud walls, passed through a gate and then walked into a second compound.

Actually it felt more like a field, it was so vast. Tall walls surrounded the land, which was divided up by irrigation channels into squared plots planted with vegetables, flowers, and fruit trees. There was a simple house near the river but we ate outside on mats on the ground and slept on rope beds outside. The night was cool, with the roar of the river and the bright stars overhead.

The river flowed south and came down to the north side of the walls and then bent around to the east. Looking north, due to the slope of the valley, you could lie on your back and see over the walls, and it seemed that the river was flowing toward, into us. It gleamed and flicked metallic in the star and moon light.

As this was tribal area, there was always an edge of uncertainty.

We were sleeping outside, but within a huge walled compound, and there were armed men about always keeping an eye open—in case. Our hosts were striking young men and very polite, in gleaming white perani tombans (Baggy pants and long shirt). They were also very curious.

The next day we crossed the bridge over the Pech River and had our documents carefully checked at the government checkpoint. The government soldiers with their heavily fortified base seemed restricted, ill at ease—they didn't venture far, surrounded as they were by armed tribesmen who roamed freely and who everyone knew relished a good fight, especially with the central government. Here we turned left along the north bank of the river. We were on a very bad gravel rock road alongside this rushing river. It was below us, but it seemed as if our road was just part of the riverbed. The slopes were bare of trees, although trees began higher up.

Logs tore down the river or at times jammed it, logs that would float down the rivers to mills in Pakistan. All this was illegal, but . . . . Occasionally a log-cantilevered walking bridge would span the river, elegant in its narrowness and daring in its length. Houses here all had high walls and heavy gates. We stopped at a settlement to pick up our guide, Mahmoud. A discussion developed concerning armed guards. It was proposed that six to eight or more armed men come up with us to ensure our safety.

I felt this would look like a war party, and would invite undue attention. Mahmoud said he was enough. Fortunately we all agreed. Off we went, over a road that only got worse and worse. At one point we suddenly began driving as fast as we could.

Later they explained that Abdul's family had a dispute with the people owning this land and it was best that we not be observed. So we bumped and rumbled on. Eventually we stopped at a teahouse where we would leave the road and take a trail next to the river. It was adobe, with a porch in front and a balcony on the second floor, brown wood and brown mud, along a river that poured down a narrow valley from the mountains to the north. Mahmoud went in to check it out, returned and said it was OK for us to go in. I couldn't help feeling I was in an ol' cowboy movie. At this point it was decided that Mystery would leave with the jeep and return at an appointed time in a few days. Abdul, Mahmoud, my two friends, and I would head north along the river towards Azziz's village. When the "motor" left, a sense of our isolation entered in. Here we were, miles away from a seemingly besieged government outpost, starting out on a trail that really was not a trail but just the side of the river. No government, no law, no telephone, no doctors as we knew them. Now we were in tribal lands and subject to the norms and ways of their world.

This river was also rapid and silvery with occasional logs floating by. There were a few small compounds on the hillsides. But it was mostly river, fields, a compound then scrub-covered steep slopes, with wooded mountains above and beyond, where the river came from. This side of the country was hit by monsoon from the sub-continent. This plus the high altitudes brought the rains and snows that supported lusher vegetation. However, as we kept noticing, deforestation by the Pashtuns was changing the ecology. The river valley bottoms were inhabited by them now. The Nuristanis had been pushed up into the higher mountain slopes. Pashtuns were very involved in the illegal timber cutting. Nuristanis opposed it. Up was green, down was brown and bare except for irrigated fields.

On and up we went; eventually our valley narrowed and a side valley came in from the eastern mountains. We stopped here, and Mahmoud explained that we would go that way. Here grass covered the ground, and trees grew everywhere naturally, not irrigated, so green! It was so refreshing to be where all this grew wildly and so lushly, where it was not the creation of man that had to be tended by canals and frequent digging and irrigation.

Our trail up the valley was sometimes a trail, a bare earthen path, other times it was the side of an irrigation ditch that had laboriously been dug into a hillside. Once, we were on such a narrow wall and one of our party slipped, his body pressing the steep slope sides, his hands on the grass on the side of the trail. "I'm all right," he said. "No you're not," we countered as we helped him up. The slope he was on ended a ways past his feet, and it was a sharp drop amid boulders to the stream below.

We were in thick forest, but it was a bit dry because it faced south and west. On northern- or eastern-facing slopes it was denser, and higher up the dark green of conifers took over until the tree line, and then rocks and snow. Some slopes were rock, cliffs, and too steep for much tree life. Huge trees, centuries old, shaded our path; wild grapes and vines climbed up and over. Greens of many shades were everywhere.

Mahmoud was always ahead of us—scouting. Sometimes we'd see him way ahead; sometimes he was on a ledge above us, or up a tree whistling. He was playful but clearly competent and a reassuring presence with his knowledge of the terrain and his rifle. At one point we heard him talking, and higher-pitched voices answering; then we heard the tinkle-tinkle of little bells. A group of Nuristani women passed us, going downhill chatting away and laughing. The sound of bells was to ward off bears, he explained. These women were unescorted and unveiled, hair uncovered. They wore dark colors, and were happily amused by meeting foreigners on their trail; they were not shy. They wore full skirts and puttees, leg wrappings, like the men's, for protection from brambles.

There were small grassy clearings cut by brooks. From our shaded paths they seemed lit up in neon green. Further up these clearings were leveled into small, terraced, irrigated fields of rice and corn. We walked on the sides of them and then up the slopes to the next one.

We came across intricately carved structures that looked like flat roofed wood cabins. These were old tombs, we were told, from the time before the people were forced to convert. Across the path from them were square wooden platforms jutting from the hillside. They had raised bench seats and rail backs on three sides. These, we were told, were for resting. But being across from the tombs you surmised that they originally had something to do with funerary rites. Some of the carved surfaces and beams were very worn perhaps because they were just naturally gnarled, may have been used because if you looked at them for a while they started to look like creatures. We rested at these places.

It was still hot in the sun, but in the shade it was very pleasant. The air was crystal clear and scented by the vegetation. We came to the base of a steep slope and could see a flat-roofed wooden village perched high above on the cliff-like slope, house above house. And here we saw stones arranged in steps up the hillside. There was such care taken in arranging and obviously maintaining the steps—I had not seen anything like it before in the country.

The steps snaked between boulders and trees. At the top we were greeted by some of the headmen, who invited us for tea. The village seemed deserted—people were out working. The houses were squarish, flat-roofed, made of horizontal logs daubed with clay. Stacked up the hillside like steps, the roof of one was a sort of porched living area of the house above. Large logs with deep notches leaned against the walls and functioned as stairs to the next level. We walked across these roofs to a room on the edge of the settlement.

Seated inside on the floor on mats, we were offered tea. There was a low glassless window next to us, and as I poked my head out, I noticed that there was a sheer drop below us. From what we could make out of the conversation between our guides and the Nuristanis, they were laughing and comparing raids that each party had made against each other. Yes, your father came and stole our cows. Oh, yes, and your grandfather was a great warrior, he had many successful raids. This went on for some time and we grew uncomfortable with the underlying tone. Perhaps they sensed this and suggested that we sit outside as they concluded some business.

The roofs had railings on the edge that you could lean against. We sat, backs to a sheer drop behind us looking at the village, which looked like a series of steps made for giants. Higher up were the deep dark forests and rock peaks. Back down the valley we could see the narrow valleys we had come up and ranges to the south, each drier than the next, progressively drier and more barren, the Afghanistan we were familiar with. Mahmoud signaled that it was time to go. We said our goodbyes. The terrain greened further as we climbed, the tiny fields lusher, and the mountains steeper.

Up, up, the trail came to a steep slope and we could barely make out the village high up in the trees far above us. We again saw stairs and began to climb. Suddenly we heard a commotion and gradually saw a group of very animated men coming down the steps. By the tone of their voices, they were angry. We stopped. As they approached we could see one man, hatless with a bloodied head. Abdul and Mahmoud seemed alarmed.

It turned out that the wounded man was Azziz. Everyone seemed to know everyone, and Azziz recognized me from the bus. Word had been sent through people who traveled that we were coming. Our plan had been to meet him in this, his village—he was the khan there, a leader—and then go up further and deeper into Nuristan. But he had a gashed head. The story goes that just an hour or so before we arrived, he had been walking alone, and a Pashtun up the slope had dropped a rock down on his head. It did not kill him but the gash was deep.

We offered our medical supplies. But he refused. He apologized but said he could not join us because he was going down to Assadabad to see the governor about this. He was angry and adamant that the government do something about the situation. This attempted murder was part of a longstanding conflict over trees between the highland Nuristanis and the valley-dwelling Pashtuns. Over the years the Nuristanis had been pushed further and further up into the mountains.

In these days wood was in great demand. As we had seen, the rivers were full of logs floating their way to Pakistan. Simply put, some of the Pashtuns were stripping the land of trees and selling them off. It was forbidden to export wood from the country. This law was sometimes extended to wooden furniture and handcrafts, with comic, ironic results. But these logs crossed the border with ease thanks to generous payoffs. We had seen the mountains shaved clear, and were told that forests had reached as far as Assadabad even twenty years ago.

The Nuristanis, on the other hand, believed that the trees should be used but that it should all be done carefully, judiciously. They were trying to save their forests. They clearly saw the ecological disasters of the lowlands and wanted no part of it, even for money. So warfare would break out between the two groups. Azziz's bashed head was a skirmish in this contest. As a group of men were going with him to press his case, there was no one who could lead us further inland. And this was the end of Mahmoud's territory.

Many Pashtuns had a fear of Nuristan. Many stories were told and retold of the old days when, to show his manhood, a Nuristani youth had to go down and return with the head of a Pashtun. So our trip was curtailed. We were invited to stay at the village but cautioned not to venture around as there were probably other assassins in the area. There might be other problems. The village was under a kind of siege. We decided to take up the invitation to stay and to follow their advice not to go further.

We said our goodbyes and we climbed up. We climbed up, up to the village. Much larger than the other, it had the same stepped construction but we also saw peaked thatched structures off to the side; they brought to mind a Polynesian village. These were used as barns. We were brought to one home and settled in. The home had a carved central doorway and two small windows to either side. The dim interior was divided by four carved central posts, which divided the interior into nine visual areas—like a tic-tac-toe board. We learned that traditionally these areas reflected the division of labor and rank. Certain people were allowed in certain areas, and certain functions were performed in certain areas. Fire was in the center. Clearly this was an ancient tradition. Unlike the rest of the country, stools and low chairs were used here. We spent our time and ate and slept outdoors. Many rooftops were covered with food drying on mats. Again, since people were working, it all seemed half deserted. Some of the young men showed us around.

Past some terraces we came to the ruins of an old temple. In the old days at seasonal festivals, large carved effigies of figures on horseback were sung to polyphonically as people danced in circles. Their culture was quite distinct from those of the surrounding peoples. From a distance we heard high-pitched singing and it neared us. We watched as a line of women came down the trail around the edge of the terrace. They were all dressed in dark colors with pointed hats. Only their heads projected above the crops. When they noticed the foreigners among their friends, the singing stopped and they began talking and joking, continuing along their way. I felt again as if we were a kind of amusement for them.

The Nuristanis still preserved many aspects of their "old ways." Now the women were returning from tending their terraced fields. In spring the men do the ploughing and digging, the harder work. Then the women take over tending the crops. At home the men prepare food and look after the young children. Some have the kids on their backs, papoose style, as they work, say, grinding corn. It was a unique division of labor for this part of the world, and reflected their individuality. They impressed me with their clarity of thought and intelligence. One evening I was trying to get a small tape recorder to work as I wanted to tape their songs. One of them looked it over and quickly had it working and remembered how to control it, though he couldn't read the English labels on the buttons and had never seen one before. The music was energetic, spirited stuff, a world away from the music of their neighbors.

One felt that a person could stay here, disappear here, no one would know; and there was a pull to stay. But when it was time to leave, we returned down the mountain to the hot valley, to the teahouse, where Mystery had dropped us off. As it was late when we arrived, we stayed the night at the teahouse. There was some commotion about the foreigners spending the night. Clearly all was not well. It was partly our presence but also it turned out that Abdul was here and family enemies lived nearby. If they knew he was here, they would come. So, true to his offer of hospitality, again protection was provided. As we tried to sleep, armed men patrolled the roof and grounds—every time I awoke, I saw one moving, watching.

At daybreak we sped past the land of his enemies and reached Assadabad, which was hot, congested, busy. It felt like another world after the cool mountain villages. We said our farewells and thanked our wonderful host, Abdul, and our wonderful guide, Mahmoud. We bought seats in a small passenger truck for Jalalabad. The journey was uneventful except for when we entered a long gravel-covered stretch of land, north of the city. It was dusk and we saw the lights of another vehicle some distance behind us. It seemed to be gathering speed. Our driver became alarmed, and said something about horagis, foreigners.

The driver was sweating and the other passengers were tense. He began going faster and faster and the vehicle behind us also seemed to match our speed. The road was gravel, surrounded by rougher gravel, no other vehicles were in sight, and there was no habitation.

We raced in the dark to Jalalabad. As we neared a bridge and a military checkpoint, the vehicle behind us disappeared. Our driver stopped sweating and in typical Afghan fashion said it was all nothing—he had never been afraid.

Although it was night, it was still very hot. We got off at a house turned hotel that we had stayed at when we were in town. I was dreaming of a shower to wash away all the dirt and dust. In most houses water is pumped up to water drums on the roof and then flows down as needed. I got in the shower area and turned on the cold water thinking that the water should be warm after sitting up on the roof all day. I jumped out; the water was scalding hot, and remained so no matter how long I let it run.

Back in Kabul, walking down the street seemed unreal—it felt to be a different world where everyone followed a script. I felt that I had come from and been in a world that was real, where one was alive, present: mountain, people, trees, water—so exotic compared to the dusty, noisy city. I understood the Kuchis better now. These nomadic people said they were free, they were "people." Beings who lived on settled farms or in towns or cities were limited, they said; they were not "developed."

The idea of the city dweller as a weak being now made more sense. And I was only in Kabul, not in a major world city. The city seemed unclear—sure, the air was dustier; there were many, many more people, animals, and vehicles, but the clearness that was missing had something to do with the eyes. Here they were cloudier, distracted, and preoccupied. The eyes and the individual didn't seem to connect. Up there the eyes and the persons seemed to be one.

During the Soviet occupation Nuristan was bombed again and again and firebombed to destroy the tree cover. It was a major route for mujahideen supplies. They set up their own autonomous government with their own passports. Reports are that huge areas were deforested, and continue to be.

People? Abdul was tortured by the Soviet apparatus but eventually released without finger- or toenails and is safe. Mystery was killed in fighting. Gentle Mahmoud—one day a huge Soviet helicopter gunship landed by his village. The men and boys were rounded up. A large hole was dug. All the men and boys were thrown into the hole and buried alive.

These days the area conservative. It is said this is because the Nuristanis were late in becoming Muslims. They did not have the long tradition of Sufi saint tombs or Sufi mysticism, music, and zikrs, or spiritual exercises. This area fit more neatly into the Wahhabi / Salafi puritanical group ideologies. It is shocking to see the news and the dramatic films about the U.S. outposts in the Korengal Valley, the scene of intense fighting documented in the movie *Restrepo*. This is a Pashtun area south of the Pech River where this walk in Nuristan took place.

## ❧ 9 ❧

# Poplars

At the break of spring all was still drab but you could smell the change coming. They would sell flower seedlings and trees on the street. Afghans are passionate about flowers and gardens. Men would walk around with trees over their shoulders—sometimes tall trees, like poplars, reaching fifteen to twenty feet in length. What was odd was that the trees usually had no root ball; the roots were bare, just as they would be when pulled up out of the ground. It was a comment to the energy of spring and to the tremendous fertility of the soil that once planted and watered, they would grow.

Poplar trees are valued for their use as beams, straight and unbending, and because they are so fast growing, they are planted densely, like a crop. They often lined irrigation canals as did mulberry trees, which were often cut back, pollarded: for firewood, fruit for food, and leaves for silkworms.

Once in Bamiyan on a walk to the third smaller Kakrak Buddha past the ruins of the "City of Screams" I walked in a poplar field. When the Mongols were besieging it, a princess of the city wishing to save her life opened a gate. But this did not spare the city. It was destroyed in revenge for the death of a favored Mongol prince during the siege. I walked on the trails made on the top of canal walls, past fields of potatoes, wheat, and poplars. The poplars were planted as close as corn. A ditch between, each row perhaps twenty feet or more tall. I began to walk down a row. It was narrow, almost a wall of white tree trunks on each side giving way to a green, leafy canopy and glimpses of the intense blue high altitude sky. It was dark and cool and damp. I walked and walked, no end in sight, and then I began to think of perhaps backtracking, but that was far. Ahead I could see only these parallel rows diminishing into a vague, distant blur. To the left side I could see the end of the field a few rows away. But it was impossible to squeeze between the trees. Trees do not bend as corn. So like a prisoner between rows of poplars I went on until the rows ended, and emerged from the dense lush trees into the blazing sun and barren, unwatered land.

Sometimes these trees were planted in very creative, playful ways. In the garden of the ruined old royal palace in Jalalabad, burned down during the revolt against the modernizing King Amanollah in 1928, there was such a planting. Two rows of poplars were planted in large concentric circles less than a shoulder width apart. The outer circle had one break in it; there you could enter into the narrow way between the rows. Then you had to walk almost to the other side to find the opening through the inner circle of trees.

This passage was shaded and cool, it was impossible to squeeze between the trees so you kept walking in the shade, relieved to be out of the sun. But gradually this relief gave way to tension as you began to feel that there was no way in to the inner circle. And as you started to become alarmed that you might have to walk back to the beginning, you suddenly came to the break in the inner row of trees. And once through you were in a large, shady, circular space-room walled by straight white-barked trees that higher up bushed out into vivid green and that surrounded the dazzling circle of bright blue above—brown earth, white wall of tree trunks, then green wall, then the intense blue dome-like sky.

Here you felt a surge of joy at the magical open space, supremely elegant in simplicity and light and also a sense of secret privacy, of safety within these living walls. But this feeling, like so much in this country, then flipped to the opposite. The sense of safety then brought about the realization that there was only one way out, the same circular, narrow way one came in. One now felt trapped. The *qalas*, the huge abode fort-like homes, were like this too. There was only one massive gate in. If an attack came you could only fight.

## ๑ 10 ๑

# Within Ten Years the Soviets Will Come . . . .

O
ne day in the early 1970s Nur Agha and I were sitting in the garden and talking about the weather and how at certain points in the year the weather patterns would shift. It was midsummer and it had been hot. But there was a wind last night and now he said the nights would be much cooler. And it was true. Then he suddenly asked, "Do you know what is going to happen here?" We had spoken before about his plans for the future and also what he wanted to happen in the country. But today he was somber and subdued.

We were seated facing north. He gestured with his head in that direction. I knew what that meant; it was full of potent meaning, and it unsettled me. He was gesturing to the north, toward the Soviet Union. He knew of its history and of the general experience of people who didn't fit into the Soviet mold. He had Turkmen and Uzbek and Tajik friends and disciples whose families had fled purges and famines and persecutions as well as cultural subjugation under Russian and Soviet "superiority." Central Asian peoples are vividly aware of their long and illustrious history, and they deeply resented being told they must say their Russian "big brother" was superior. He knew his history too, of the expansion of the old Czarist Russian Empire into Asia, into Siberia, the taking of the Central Asian

States one by one, Ukraine, the Baltic States, Poland, and of the continuation of this policy under the Soviet Empire. The magnitude of WWII, the Holocaust, and Stalin's horrors were well known to him. He knew, too, of some of my relatives' experiences in Nazi camps and the Soviet Gulag camps. My family had immigrated to America from Eastern Europe in 1910. So when he gestured, it was not just a movement of the head. It was a movement full of portent, of one historical tide hitting against another, a clash of centuries. And we both knew what that had cost so far in human terms.

On the surface, Afghanistan was independent, and the people fiercely so. But the Soviet Union trained the military and had massive development projects, the vast majority of which were financed by loans. Ninety percent of Soviet aid, much larger than U.S. aid, was in the form of loans, while the majority of U.S. aid was through grants.

There was a push from every country to portray itself favorably to the Afghan government. It was all part of the Cold War game, and the Afghans viewed themselves as experts in milking these various "cows." Each nation publicized its own projects. And Afghans would respect a country based on its projects, whether they were good and whether they actually worked. The large airport outside Kandahar was built by the U.S. to serve as a major world service stop for prop airplanes. Now, with jets, it was outdated, but because it brought prestige to the city and area, it was still valued, whereas bridges built by some countries that were destroyed in the periodic flash floods were not. On top of these projects, some nations built schools or cultural centers fostering their language, such as the French Lycée, the Germans, the Americans. Everyone did this and everyone tried to win favor with various Afghan leaders, offering trips, scholarships, gifts of liquor, bribes and occasionally other pleasures, and so on.

Nur Agha said the Russians are coming; they will be here within ten years. I believed what he said—he was privy to a lot of information that I, of course, didn't have and didn't want. He was a religious leader but because of the respect people held him in, he also had a lot of power, and people came to him. And on an intuitive level I felt what he said to be true. I knew the history, and as the old Russian Empire was based on expansion it had wanted access to the warm seas, so too did the Soviet Union.

I asked, "What will happen?" picturing in my mind men with guns in adobe villages firing at the hard steel of the Soviet Red Army machine.

"They will fight."

"But do they know the power of a modern army? One bomb, and a whole village will be gone. The whole country will be destroyed."

Nur Agha said, "You know this, and I know this, but they don't know this and they do not care. They will fight on and on, until the Soviets are gone."

I said it would all be destroyed—I pictured bombers blowing the country to smithereens. He reached down and picked up some earth. "It is *khok*, dust; the buildings are made of dust, adobe. The country will be destroyed and then it will be rebuilt." He was not happy, but very heavy, just stoic and heavy. I was being rational. Nur was a Sufi Sheikh who did exercises to explore consciousness. And he was just stating what the people would do, and he was also expressing his anguish, describing what would come. That was in 1973. The Soviets came in the late '70s. And the Afghans did just fight on and on, ignoring staggering losses, that would have stopped most countries. Possibly two million dead vs. 15,000 Soviet. They just fought on and on against the machine and, after the Soviets left, as if they could not stop, against each other.

# ৩ 11 ৩

# Parwon Nace, Inshallah, Dek, Dewaneh, and Shahid

I dioms and proverbs are great keys to understanding the thinking and psychology of a language and people. Once you get the way a language feels, then you can really use it. People study languages, say, English, and so many people, and heads of state use it. Yet native speakers and those who have really learned a language stand out.

They do not "use" the language; they are "in" it. Their eyes, gestures, body language clearly reveal fluency; a word that itself refers to flowing. You can tell people's fluency by their body language. For instance, Nami, a Japanese speaker, does not have the same body language as, say, Jairo, from Mexico, and vice versa.

Two constantly used phrases in Dari are *parwon nace* and *Inshallah*. Parwon nace can be "it doesn't matter." If something does not work right, this is what one says. It means, "OK, I'm disappointed, but it's OK," but it also reveals the concept "So what? Nothing matters." It is used constantly to shield disappointments and more. It reflects a deep undercutting of futility—"So what if I tried, it didn't work, it doesn't matter, I can't think about it." The right to be upset with disappointment, to protest, to express hurt—sometimes these all get numbed up by this nihilistic expression. Why try . . . ?

*Inshallah* means God willing. But not, as Nur would have said, as you try, using your energy and your brain asking God's help and will. Yes, it can be used positively, but unfortunately most people use it to mean, "If God wants it, God will do it, will have to do it. I will try only so much, the rest is fate." Many would prepare only so far and then leave the remainder, invoking this phrase, as if wanting to see if God really wanted them to do it. If so, then the remainder would fall into place and that meant that God willed it and all was well. If it did not fall into place, then God did not will it so. To an outsider it seemed an abandonment of taking all the steps necessary to have something happen.

A driver of a shared taxi to another city would say, "We will leave in twenty minutes, Inshallah," and sit hoping more customers would come to fill up the car. Another person could stand outside and shout his destination, try to drum up business.

Dinner will be at eight. Of course one could plan and arrange it so—or, as usual, preparations would begin and continue until all was ready, whatever, whenever.

*Dek* is a word that means sad. It sounds simple. But it is one of these massive pillars that hold up a vast superstructure of culture. To be dek is something to be avoided at all costs. People will rush to help change your mood, as if it were contagious and that they too will get it next. They will tell jokes, cajole you, lavish attention on you, feed you. Being away from one's family would produce this state. They wonder how foreigners can be so far away for so long. Space to be an individual is not that common—one is always a part of a family, a clan, a tribe; one is usually physically close to others. The rights of the group always come first. Individuality doesn't exist as a Westerner knows it. Being sick or suffering from a broken heart were major causes of being dek.

I recall the brother of a friend was hurt in some student demonstrations. He had been stabbed by a conservative mullah. He was home, and given massive injections of various vitamins (these could be purchased from any pharmacy along with almost anything) and was never left alone. There were people by his side twenty-four hours a day, talking, visiting. I came and suggested to my friend that perhaps his brother needed to be alone, to sleep more. "No, that would make him dek and more ill, and it would make us dek. No, no."

If you were dek, it was understood by those around you that you could no longer be held accountable and responsible for all your actions. There was a leeway given you, like a safety zone where you could go and be somewhat distant from your normal life. Now there was another step beyond this. If you were *dewaneh*, you were crazy. This could mean a state of mental illness where one could not function in a normal way. Or it could mean that you were God crazy, that somehow you were touched by the Divine and could no longer function in a normal way. Or it could be a way by which one could withdraw, temporarily or permanently.

I knew of a case where a European-educated professional had his heart broken. He had been abroad for years, had studied, and had fallen in love before. But this time an Afghan love refused his marriage proposal and he became dewaneh. He stayed in his family's home for years and did very little. People visited, everyone recognized his state, and this was OK. This could happen to you because of love, or work, or whatever. Pining away for love was a massive vein in Dari/Persian literature. Everyone knew the story of Layla and Majnun, and others, doomed like Romeo and Juliet. The literature legalizes this behavior; it is a traditional way, an accepted way to be.

Thwarted love can be of two kinds, yet they are also viewed as the same. The beloved one pined for could be one's physical love, male or female. But the Beloved could also be the Lord, the God, who is there but not there. And as the literature expressed one could be intertwined with both, the physical and the spiritual. There is also the tradition of the *shahid*. This "way" says that one should follow one's physical love in whatever ways one can, even if forbidden, even if this leads to problems in society. One should, because this piece of love you are pursuing—loving a person, provided you kept a certain perspective—would be making a very great spiritual journey, whether you realize it or not. Love being a kind of yoga, you love, but watch it too. You watch as you very passionately abandon yourself, and at some level you are touching God. This is a very old tradition in every religion in some form, much denounced by conservative religious leaders.

## ∽ 12 ∾

# Careful

In my classroom one day I was standing next to the three boards painted black on the wall—the blackboard. There was a simple wooden table and chair for me. The students sat on benches in rows with an aisle down the middle. The floor was made of beautiful Afghan marble tiles, the walls dusty and unpainted for years, the windows mostly broken; the idea of maintenance in many countries is considered lowly.

This was a good class, high level, in one of the best boys' high school in Kabul. I had a book I was responsible for teaching, on which their all important tests would be based. They did not have books. Students had as many as seventeen subjects to be tested on, all done by rote memorization. I did not have paper, but could occasionally buy some. There was no chalk for the blackboards, but it was possible to find some in the bazaar.

The book series adopted by the Ministry of Education was developed by "experts," professors from Columbia University, New York City. It was another U.S.A.I.D. project. The books were a problem. For example, it dedicated a large section to the pattern; "this is a book and that is too, this is an apple and that is too, I am a student and you are too," etc. This seemed to be stressed as a major block of the English language. We volunteers all viewed it as another byproduct of the academic world. But we had to teach it as it would be on the all important tests. We all also tried to teach real English.

Today's lesson involved adjectives, such as "beautiful," "wonderful" . . . . Although they were beyond this level I asked if they knew the word *beautiful*; yes, they said, and they gave examples. I went on and then came to the word *careful*. I asked if they knew this word, several snickered. My mind began to race, the word seemed below their level yet they reacted with silence and nervousness or various degrees of snickering. I said, "take care of." If someone is sick you take care of them, you prepare food, get medicine, and take care of.

Now some covered their mouths and began to laugh, trying hard not to and trying hard to hide it. I thought I've got to get this word across to them somehow. The more examples I gave the more they snickered or laughed. Someone shouted that they knew "care."

"Good," I said, and they laughed, and I, more confused than anything said OK.

So what is careful? You know care. Now "full" means a lot of inside, like eating and your mouth is full of food. And I puffed up my cheeks to portray a full mouth. They laughed more. I used other examples, a full pocket, a full box, a full briefcase. They laughed. I asked do you understand careful? Azziz said, "Yes," and pointed to the student at his side and said, "he is careful." They laughed and laughed. Confused, I said, "how do you know he is careful?" He answered; "I know, I saw." The laughing and tense snickering and hiding ones face now gave way to rolls of laughter. This was in sharp contrast to the blank look on my face. I was embarrassed: I had lost control of the class; was amused yet deeply lost in the chaos of it all, yet it felt good natured. I never felt seriously mocked in the country.

The bell rang, I was saved, and retreated to the all-male teachers 'room, where I confided what I have tried to teach. They then began to laugh and laugh hysterically and carry on. They kept repeating the word "care." It was a while before anyone was able to stop laughing long enough to explain things to me. I learned that the word "care" sounds like the Dari word for penis.

# 🕭 13 🕮

# Farah Home

Nur Agha told me that several tribes of Baluch, inhabitants of southern Afghanistan, southwestern Pakistan, and southeastern Iran, were interested in getting title to good land that they could farm. They were known for their wonderful rugs and complete honesty. This was before the wars and massive drug smuggling. This group, some five thousand families, now semi-nomadic, wanted land in the southwest on the Farah Rud, the Farah River, where it crosses the major road to Herat. The river was good sized and flowed all year long. They could irrigate.

They went to the government, they were greeted well, their request was recorded, but nothing resulted from these meetings. They asked various people to speak for them, but with the same results. Then they turned to Nur Agha and asked him to be their spokesperson.

He met with the government and was told that everything was under consideration. He was also told that as in many projects in the country, the Communist embassies had an input and the Western embassies had theirs. Soviet advisors strongly urged that the tribes be dismantled and that everyone be settled down on "happy" collective farms, just like in the Soviet Union. American advisors, on the other hand, advised that the tribal structures also be dismantled but that the people be settled down on small family farms, like in the West.

He asked me what I thought, and we had great discussions. I said that collectivization had been installed in the USSR by force, with millions dead. First the intelligentsia was murdered then the artificial famines to break the will of the people, as in Kazakhstan and Ukraine in 1932–33, with millions more perishing in camps. There was strong evidence that the Soviet model did not work. We also saw the American proposal as unrealistic. How do you divide clans into small families—who would they go to for help? We felt that both models did not reflect Afghan realities. It was clear that the people had very limited resources and that government help would be limited. It would be mostly up to them to develop the land.

So Nur Agha went to the king. His family, his father had been so respected that the king would come to him. Nur Agha wanted the king to grant the Baluchi tribes title to the land and allow them to settle down in tribal groupings. His argument was that within their established tribal structures they already knew how to cooperate and work together. They would be able to pool their resources to buy tractors and seed and the implements they would need, and to build the shelters and irrigation works they would require. This plan reflected our discussions.

He added that he would buy two thousand *jeribs* of land (about 988 acres) to develop as an experimental farm and home. He was very interested in modern agriculture and was eager to work with government advisors and farmers to develop the systems necessary in this new land venture. He said that because of his religious standing, the people would follow his suggestions before those of Kabul "expert" agriculture advisors.

The king reportedly was pleased with this solution since it followed neither a Soviet nor a Western model, but was Afghan instead.

Nur Agha was very happy with his project. His eyes widened every time he spoke of this possibility or that, of his new home. He wanted to distance himself from the activities of his family and others and wanted to establish his own center there in Farah. He would teach Sufism, farm, and help the people to develop their abilities.

One day he said, "Out of my land I am giving you fifty jeribs. I will wall it off for you, and I will terrace it and irrigate it, and build a domed adobe home, and I will plant orchards in it, and take care of it for you. But it will be yours. The income from the crops will eventually pay for its development costs. You can live there every time you come to Afghanistan. It will be next to my house. It will be your home."

I was shocked and deeply, deeply happy with his very generous gift. I could actually have my dream domed house and have a garden. I felt, yes, I would always have a home in Afghanistan.

But the wars came as he foretold. He and all his family fled to Pakistan. The Baluchi fought and have tried to survive. He passed away.

## ๑ 14 ๑

# A Woman Beats the British:
# Women and the Veil

Yes, men and women were separated. Yes, women were often unapproached, veiled, secluded, but this did not always mean what it seemed to mean.

On July 27, 1880, on the plains of Maiwand near Kandahar, a brigade of the Imperial British Army faced a large Afghan force. A battle commenced, but the Afghan line broke, and retreat began, and then total chaos—everyone fleeing back towards Kandahar. A lone Afghan woman, a new bride, was seen walking towards the British lines. Her people yelled for her to flee, that she was going the wrong way. She answered that she was going to fight the English because there were no men left in the country to do it. The men—shamed—regrouped, charged, and the British Army suffered one of their most crushing losses. This led to the resolution of the Second Afghan British War and semi-independence.

In the old days only the wealthy women wore chadors, or *burqa*, the pleated tent-like covering that fits over the head. Everyone else had to work—long scarves were more practical in the fields. In recent times conservative families used the chador, then some new middle class or village people, who recently moved to the cities and styled themselves on the old elite, wore it. They wanted to be "in" to show that they had arrived, to show that their women did not have to work.

Ironically the elite, the middle classes, and educated classes largely discarded it then in favor of simple head scarves, babushkas, with the hair showing.

The chador, or burqa, has a mesh net grill that you look through that limits your vision and your ability to observe what is coming from behind you, like a car, truck, or man. It fits over the head snugly and falls down in tiny pleats. This narrow-pleated material was later taken up by French designers and is still seen in dress fashions.

In order to see as clearly as possible a woman needs to pull and hold down the material below the net with her covered hand so that the net is flush against her face and does not billow out. Crossing streets she has to keep turning her head side to side to stay aware of traffic and movement. It takes a lot of energy and focus to keep peering out, to keep holding the mesh down, to keep the rest of the chador from billowing out, to keep looking intently at what is happening around you, and to also keep looking down so that you know where to step and where not to. And if you were carrying groceries or holding the hand of a child it was very difficult.

If you have poor vision, it is harder of course, and if you wear glasses underneath, it is much more awkward. You could see a chadored woman step into traffic, and cars swerve and drivers yell and the woman would sometimes freeze, or would try to run back. Sometimes it reminded me of a deer caught in the headlights of a car, wanting to run but half-paralyzed with fear or incomprehension.

It was odd too to hear a voice coming out from underneath this veil to bargain with a shopkeeper. It sounded several steps removed from the present. Of course this covering brought a whole different psychological way of living. It also brought anonymity, a secret kind of freedom. Even men use it when in need, to escape.

Now there, and everywhere around the world, Wahhabis, Salafis and other rigid but extremely well-funded groups are promoting veiling. The moderate groups seem silent.

Supporters of its use say that, more than providing anonymity, it preserves a woman's modesty. Some say a woman's hair is private, that it and a woman's beauty arouse a man's lust—thus the veil. I've heard the women say if men have such problems, then since they are the ones with the problem, they should be veiled or restrained or controlled in some way.

The debate is for them to sort out; it is their world. But it should be based on choice, and rarely does the woman have the full power and awareness to choose for herself. It is usually husband, family, group pressure—fear. But it did seem that the more separated the sexes were, the more veiled and rigid, then the greater the sexual frustration and the greater the tensions. Surely the modern dressed Afghans of those former days, who worked together, seemed more relaxed about it; it just was not such a big deal.

I remember a woman who wore a scarf when outside stared at me when I asked her what she thought about the chador. She looked at me as if she didn't understand what I was saying. She said, in English, "I hate that thing," but added that her mother wore it and felt afraid if she didn't have it on. But she said she had done that all her life and that she was old. "But once you take it off, you never want to go back". It's the men who force the women . . ." I asked many others, and the answers were all similar.

When I got to know Nur Agha, I asked him why the women in his family did not wear the chador. He looked very irritated with the idea. He said the women in his family going all the way back almost a thousand years were never veiled. He said it was not a rule of Islam. Islam stressed modesty, he insisted. Things like the chador were cultural. He said this is a big problem for the religion. In many countries people did things that they swore was part of their religion, but actually they were only traditions of their own people, their own culture. They were not part of the religion. He seemed tired when he explained these points to me. He said he would teach until all his hair turned white, but he was not sure how many people listened.

He said "modesty is modesty"—it means not to attract attention to oneself. He asked me which would attract more attention in the West, a chadored woman or a woman in a bikini. I said it depended on the woman, but it would be pretty close. Then he asked which would attract more attention, a woman in hijab, the wrap-around head covering so "in" these days with young Muslims, or just a normal Western-dressed woman I said of course the veiled woman would always provoke more attention, people "look." "Yes," he said. In Western societies the veiled woman was the source of attention: people look—this is *fitr*, an Arabic word for scandal. I saw his point. He said modesty is modesty; you do not draw undo attention to yourself. He added that he had heard that women in the West were not subject to the street harassment common there. I answered that it was so. He said, "See, even less reason for all that covering." He added that the burqa worn in other countries made no sense and just provoked anti-Islamic feelings.

Nur Agha said people don't like to think—thinking is work. They prefer the easy way—to just follow some rules, or traditions, or because everyone else does something, or because it gives some power. He said unfortunately people use the Qur'an every which way. The chador, the veil, was just such a case, he said. This interpretation of modesty became institutionalized, and then, as he said, you saw chadors in not just somber tones but in bright colors—a seeming contradiction.

Of course the chador became absolute law under the Taliban. The Taliban-allied conservative leader Hekmatyar and the Northern Alliance leader Rabbani, are both said to have thrown acid in the faces of women they felt were immodestly attired. No wonder the chador, now called by the non-Afghan name burqa, is around.

# A Party

I was invited to a dinner. They were people who would not be hurt financially by offering a dinner, so I accepted. Many people offered invitations but one knew that families would go for a month without meat just to be able to offer meat to a guest. So one had to be careful. They said seven, which meant around eight. So I came at seven thirty with flowers—yes, I had to be careful what colors I chose, different colors send different messages—and was early. We sat in the Western-style living room and waited for the others.

Black or green tea, or "coka" or "fonta" soda were offered along with plates of nuts, raisins, and *nokle*, almonds or apricot pits covered with small drops of sugar. The apricot pits were a cheaper substitute for almonds, but I loved them—the contrast of slightly bitter with sweet. *No khoot*, dried chickpeas, were a boon as they helped one not go to the bathroom that often. It was always a bit embarrassing to ask to go out.

Old forms of politeness were observed—one never blew one's nose in the presence of others—you went outside. They use two fingers to do it. Blowing your nose is akin to defecating. You can imagine the horror as they observe horagis, foreigners, using handkerchiefs and then returning them to their pockets!

There were all sorts of poetic idioms used when you needed to use the WC—"Please, I have to go to the answer to the tea?" Some people were embarrassed that they did not have a Western-style one. It was usually the raised outhouse, raised so that it could be shoveled out through the small opening street-side. It was carried away by donkeys and made into "night soil," fertilizer. A staple of all old cultures, here it was used to grow vegetables in and near the city. Very ecological, but also because it sometimes was not aged and processed correctly, it contributed to the spread of microorganisms and disease, giardia, amoeba —thus, no salads; uncooked leafy plants were not safe.

We used Western utensils. In traditional settings, one used one's right hand. The left one was reserved for toilet functions and was judged unclean, thus you always used the right hand in handling things. One could use one's left hand to help pass things or to help tear bread into smaller pieces, but never to eat with. A ewer was brought and warm water was poured from it over one's hands into a bowl with a pierced-work cover, then a white towel to dry one's hands.

Out came huge old Chinese plates covered with Kabuli pilau— rice, carrot shreds, raisins, almonds, and saffron rice concealing pieces of meat or chicken inside, and naan, the delicious whole wheat flat bread. After offering and refusing and offering and refusing various dishes, our meal was done. The room was cleared and eventually trays of tea, sugar, and hard candy were brought out. One could add sugar to tea or keep a piece of candy in one's mouth and allow that to sweeten the tea as one drank. Cookies and baklava were brought out. The latter was similar to the international version but since most, if not all, the ingredients were organic and fresh—the taste was very wonderful.

As we joked and told stories, several people left the room and each returned carrying a musical instrument. A pair of tablas was brought out. These North Indian drums were popular in Kabuli culture. Their deep resonating beats fit well with the echoing sound of

Kabuli music. Most of the country used a simple "under the arm" kind of drum—played with both hands. There were various folk music systems in the country reflecting the various languages and cultures.

Then there were the old classical musical systems, one from Iran, one from Bukhara in Central Asia, and those from North India. Ragas from India were sung but with a more vigorous style than in their homeland. Music is a basic element of all the various Afghan cultures. Radios and tapes are always blaring and people are always ready to sing. A group of men sitting on the top of a bus might mark their departure by suddenly clapping hands and starting a song, some moving their hands as if they were dancing. Of course nowadays the Taliban have their own interpretations of Islam and have banned music.

Beside the tabla, in came a *rebab*, a classical stringed instrument with some fretted strings and more sympathetic strings that simply vibrated to the others. It was deeply carved out with two indentations, made of mulberry wood, skin, with the neck usually inlaid with mother-of-pearl. It has a deep rich sound. Also came a harmonium, of North Indian influence, a small hand pumped organ. Sometimes they used a *tambura*—a long stringed instrument from India. It was held upright, its many strings played to create a drone, and sometimes a *richak/ghidjak*—an upright type of violin, and a *tambur*, or *dotar* or *seytar*—a long necked lute with a few strings common to many neighboring countries.

Many Afghans could play at least one instrument and all could sing.

The old excuse "I can't sing" was not accepted. Because one didn't have to follow just the rigid "do, re, mi, fa, so, la, ti" system, introduced in Western Europe only some four hundred years ago. One could sing in the voice one's body had, the natural human way. There are allowances made for variations in voice. Some sing deep or shrill, or dissonantly; it is all OK, it is from the heart. And as anyone familiar with music around the world it all works, in America—country, gospel, and jazz.

Having music in the home—playing, singing, and dancing—was natural. In modern households these parties were mixed, men and women. In conservative ones, each sex had their own. As the musicians tuned up, people began urging each other to sing, complimenting, praising, threatening. Everyone, of course, declined, swore they were no good, had no talent. Finally one was physically pushed up.

We were seated on chairs and sofas or on cushions on the ever red carpets. The musicians, as traditional, sat on the carpeted floor. The drums began, then the instruments introduced the form and melody of the piece, and then the singer. Pieces went on for some time. Some were purely instrumental. Just as people were urged, pushed, cajoled into singing, so now they were urged to dance. Initially they declined, but as before, they soon complied with relish. One person would stand up and begin as the musicians played and everyone else clapped hands in time. Although everyone had stated they couldn't, or simply had no ability, so too everyone performed, sang, or danced well, very well.

As with so many things in the country, you could see the remnants, the elements of a former very refined court life. Just as Dari, the form of Persian used in Afghanistan, literally means "the language of the court," so in music and dance, echoes of the past remained. To dance you raised your heels and focused weight on the front of your feet, and gingerly moved them, arms high and out, almost like a bird. Your hands and arms gestured seductively or expressively. Often one hand would be palms or fingers pointing up, and the other hand would be palms or fingers pointing down. This, like the music, literature, almost everything, reflected the fact that things could be interpreted secularly or spiritually. Just as in the

Old Testament Psalms in the Bible, the Song of Songs, or the writings of Christian mystics, the love expressed could be to one's lover or to God. In this case, the up and down gestures referred to Sufi dervish dancing or whirling, the person being a pole or *qutb*, connecting heaven above and earth below.

At this party people danced, alone and also together, women with women, and men with men. It was rhythmic and also gorgeous, graceful dancing. It was seductive, but had little of the more sexy western Asian belly or Arabic dancing (when I lived in Iran and went to my first party there, I was shocked by the level of sexuality). Everyone danced beautifully, and then an older gentleman was urged to dance. Everyone praised his dancing. At first demeaning and deprecating his own skills, he eventually got up, stood on the balls of his feet, extended his arms, one open hand upwards, the other downwards, and slowly, in sync with the beat, moved ever so slowly, yet every move was totally with the expression of the music. His gestures were very strong, but not vigorous. He slowly moved about the room, head tilted this way then that, coordinated with his hand gestures. Totally surrendered to the music, he did not dance to the music; he wasn't performing, he was possessed by it; he was the music.

And so, here we were in this delightful, happy dinner and party, listening, clapping to music that could be secular or spiritual. We took it as both, as one. The older man—clearly the best dancer of that evening, one of the best I have ever seen—was not performing and we all knew it and were happy. As they sang of love for the beloved, he danced to the words and surrendered, he surrendered to "the Other." So on one level, it was a party and at the same time just as the words of the song reflected the mundane and the holy so too did the party, the dancing. Some people danced performing, or enjoying each other, communicating with matching or reacting gestures—one's hand had moved forward, another's hand moved back, a step to, a retreat back.

These were conversations—coy games, matched with shy reserve or aggressive stances. Friendships, other sex or same sex, were deepened by these communications, personalities were explored, and walls raised or lowered that evening. Human beings were responding to each other in friendship part sexually, part spiritually, and more.

The party continued late. And we left a red-floored room warm with bodies and the smell of food and herbs, put our shoes back on and went outside to empty streets lined with high walls and locked gates. High, rugged, dark mountains in every direction, an occasional policeman, the frequent barking of distant packs of dogs, half wolves. High altitude stars and moon illuminated the city and valley in a silvery metallic light that made the warm tan and brown adobe walls appear velvet-like. The night was bright like the high noon of a different dimension.

Night haunts us all, but here, it was so empty, so quiet, mountain range after mountain range under a domed sky of vivid, pulsating stars that seemed beyond the count of numbers. You felt the vastness of the Central Asian world and you wanted to be warmed by people, and be again inside these walls, in warm red-floored rooms. You wanted to be emboldened and distract yourself from the awesomeness by singing songs, by music, by being next to someone.

One felt so coldly insignificant out there in the emptiness, in the night, it felt like some people's idea of religious rigidity. But the dancing man surrendered not to this domineering absolute; no, he surrendered to a song of love, to the Beloved, to his God of Love. And I remember his communion.

## ᗏ 16 ᗍ

# Nauruz

At the spring equinox, March 21, the first day of spring, the Afghans, Tajiks, Iranians, Kurds, Azerbaijanis, and others celebrate Nauroz, "new day," the New Year. Special dishes are prepared, new clothes worn, continual visits paid, and customs practiced that vary from culture to culture.

At this time, over the wall of the Hindu Kush mountains from Kabul, on the endless northern plains that stretch all the way to middle Europe, the ground turns red with a massive carpet of small red tulips. Interestingly the Turkoman carpets made in this area are of various hues of red only. This is the same flower that delighted the Turks who originated in this vastness of Central Asia and then migrated due west. It is fascinating to look at a map and see the Turkic-speaking countries and areas that stretch in a single band, reflecting migration, from western China across to modern Turkey.

The Persians and the Ottoman Turks suffused their blue tiles and fabrics and carpets with this flower's elegant design. These products in turn traveled to Europe and there found a welcome reception, with the tulip motif endlessly recreated.

This simple bulb tended and bred by devoted Ottoman horticulturalists, struck a similar response with the hugely wealthy Dutch in the 1600s. Awash in prosperity from their armadas of merchant ships plying the world trade routes, these merchants were constantly on the lookout for new products. When they came across the tulip, they were infected. This led to the "tulip fever" of the 1600s when vast fortunes were made and lost in commodity futures trading on the bare bulbs and their possible "blossom" the coming spring. The tulip fever came and went, but the tulip stayed in Holland and we know the rest.

Nauroz is Zoroastrian, and even pre- Zoroastrian, and of course, older than Islam. In the city of Mazar-e-Sharif, on this red-flowered plain there is a large shrine with the tomb of Hazrat Ali, the martyred son-in-law of the Prophet, and the fourth orthodox Caliph of Islam. Here they say that he is not buried in the Shiite complex in Najaf in Iraq but that a camel carrying his body stopped here. Eventually it was recognized and the shrine complex developed.

The building is clad in Afghan tile, much simpler, but more vibrant in color compared to Iranian tile work. In the open plaza area at Nauroz, tens of thousands of pilgrims gather to witness the raising of a huge multicolored flagpole, the Janda. It flies for forty days, a central tall pole raised at springtime—a custom of many lands, even far-off England; a very ancient symbolic fertility custom.

In a song, "Mullah Mohmad Jan", from the 1100s, revived in the 1970s, the singer, male or female, implores "Mohmad dear" to come with them to Mazar for this pilgrimage, to see the flowers: a twelfth-century Sufi song now also a love song of the twentieth century. Love expressed to a lover can also be to one's "Beloved," to God, and vice versa.

East of Mazar is Surkh Kotal, the ruins of a fire temple of the Kushans from 130 AD, a massive terraced hill, with steps climbing up in five terraces to a fire temple and white stone Greek carvings overlooking the vast plains.

Northwards on the southern bank of the Oxus River lies Ay Khanum, the ruins of a classical Greek city, whose art included a mix of Greek, Bactrian, and Persian, which came in contact with the art of India and Buddhism and fed the development of Gandharan art. The high-tech Greek statues now were of the Buddha in classical robes. These forms went north and east to China, Korea, and Japan. Nearby is Samangan, site of a Buddhist monastery, fourth to fifth century AD, and a twenty-eight-meter stupa carved out of solid rock.

Of course there are many mounds, tombs, ruins, prehistoric caves throughout the area—many unexcavated, many greatly destroyed by looting and decades of war, or, like Ay Khanum, looted and then bulldozed by the Taliban, the "goods," like so much else, sold to wealthy Asian and European dealers and sent out via Pakistan.

## ❧ 17 ❧

# Karachi Men and Students

*K*arachis* are large two-wheeled wooden carts with a projecting U-shaped bar in front. Men stood inside this U and
pushed forward on it; others might push from behind. The
men who pulled were Hazara, Mongolian-looking Shiites from the
central mountains, desperately poor.

Sometimes you would see these carts piled twenty feet high or
more—staggering loads atop a wooden platform only two by three
meters. And because of poverty, the two wheeled axel did not turn.
It could only go straight and only gradually, and with great skill
make a turn. Sometimes people made way for them; sometimes it
was survival of the fittest or cleverest. And sometimes it was like a
map of the society: nobody moved for them.

It was a cold winter day on a narrow street near what people
call Chicken Street in Shahre Naw, the new city. The street was in
shadow and was almost covered with pools of ice, and piles of snow
lined the sides. It was very cold. This being an affluent part of town,
the first floor of the buildings were shops. A bakery, fruit sellers
with oranges piled in huge pyramids, rug and antique sellers, dry
good stores, a florist.

There was little traffic, but behind me came yells and I looked
to see two men pulling a karachi laden high with what looked like
household goods. They were pulling but they were slipping on the

ice and the cart kept moving on. Their faces were strained and covered with sweat—horrible work.

There were people on the street and some of the shop keepers were at their doors chatting with each other. Then a tall man, by face he had the features of a Pashtun, turned from the buckets of flowers he was arranging in front of his florist shop. He had a pail of water in his hands. And then he swung the pail and threw the water directly on the two sweating men pulling the karachi. He laughed and yelled something at them, and then he was joined by many other shopkeepers, who also laughed and enjoyed his joke.

None of them expressed any opposition to this cruel joke. I did , but he just laughed at my comments—something about stupid foreigners. "They're just Hazara, just Shia," he said. I felt as cold as the ice-covered ground.

Educated people were always telling outsiders that they were all Afghans, all shared the same religion—no differences! But in real life there are many episodes such as this.

The karachi men? They just kept pulling their load—to try to stop was normally hard, and this was on ice. The momentum of the cart and their being inside the yoke dictated their course of action. And they were not stupid fellows; they knew they were outnumbered and that they had no support. To try to stop and confront and fight would be worse; they'd endanger their cargo, and the shop keeper had money—he could bribe the police, a judge, anyone. Besides, they were Hazara and had endured much already. They did not break stride; they kept going, with the laughter and taunts echoing behind them.

I remember another day with karachi men. It was late spring; May Day, when the weather really began to warm up and the fruit trees began to bloom, first the white almond, then the others. School had been in session for some time now. They are closed in winter—no way to heat them. One day I noticed that students were milling around outside their schools with flags and banners. All the schools, it seemed, were closed. The students were demonstrating.

We all had heard about the political parties that were forming and had heard all sorts of predictions regarding future events. Everything from a Communist revolution to attacks of conservative mountain tribesmen, to evacuation of the city, and, like the English evacuation in 1842, we would all be slaughtered on our way through the gorges out to Pakistan.

Now suddenly demonstrators were here; it was today. Exciting more than unnerving. Students were massing in the streets with banners and were heading to the city center. It was stirring to see people forming groups under banners, chanting slogans. I watched as they began to move. Foreigners were told not to go near any demonstrations. A foreign presence could be interpreted in many ways—best to stay clear.

However, later in the day I went downtown. There were several groups, identified by their banners. They were separated from each other ideologically and politically, ethnically. There were Parcham (moderate) and Khalq (hardline), pro Soviet and pro Chinese Communist groups, conservative groups, and fundamentalists, and others. The first two played leading support roles during the Soviet occupation. I moved near, but not close, going from one group to another. The air was charged with excitement, so many to observe. One scene in particular stayed in my memory.

The speakers generally stood on walls of compounds on the sides of the main streets to address their supporters. In this case, a young man, university age, was addressing a large crowd. It was near the central mosque with the blue dome by the bridge, where commercial activity became intense. He was emotional and very declarative—like a speaker of old. He was passionate and gestured dramatically. The crowd of students loved him. They responded with cheers and chants. I couldn't follow his words but shared in the energy.

It was obvious to me as he was gesturing to the bazaar and to workers and beggars by the mosque that he was addressing the difficult life many people had. Below him the crowd stood in the road. Suddenly they parted and several heavily loaded karachis came through. These karachis were of course piled high and very heavy—a merchant would want to get his money's worth; you would see a prosperous shopkeeper bargaining furiously with these desperate, worn men.

Karachis are used to move goods, store, home, anything and everything. They could negotiate the narrow alleys of the old city as well as paved areas. They could move rapidly once momentum had developed. But they had no brakes except the humans who had to judge the slope, figure a way, and use their bodies to slow or halt the often massive moving pile of goods.

These karachis came through, pulled by sweating Hazara men.

They, remnants of Genghis Khan's armies, did the brute manual labor. You could see the strain in their weathered, leathered faces as they leaned forward and pushed with all their might, and see the poverty in their ragged clothes. They strained and yelled for others to move, desperate that their momentum would not be broken or else they would have to start the cart moving all over again, and that was a great effort.

There was the crowd, students somewhat well dressed, the karachis pulled not by horse or mule, but by brute human force, the wall, and atop it educated passionate speakers. They were high school and university students, privileged people, as was most of the crowd. They spoke in high Dari, the older form of Persian, the language used by Rumi, of almost a thousand years ago, and the other classical Persian-language poets, using the high literary vocabulary, the language of their books and schools.

The laborers, as Hazara, spoke Hazaragi, their mountain version of Dari. And those that knew Dari better had, of course, a more limited vocabulary than the students. Most had never been to a school, and if they had, it was limited and consisted of memorizations.

Their words were of work, food, family, pain, farming—of practical everyday necessities. The students used ideological words, classical words, big words from their books. They were on the walls, shouting and proclaiming. They were in the crowd, cheering and chanting.

And below the people on the wall and through the crowds moved the men heaving and yelling to make way and pulling their inhumanly loaded cart. They just kept pushing and pulling their karachis on below the shouting speakers through the dense crowd on into the maze and din and dust of the crowded earth-colored old city. The high words continued uninterrupted. These working people and others in the crowds did not understand the high literary language of the demonstrators. These workers could not go to school, could not take a day off to demonstrate.

Two worlds intersecting, bisecting, but with no communication—it was a harbinger of what was to come.

## ☙ 18 ☙

# Goat

Afghans are a very hospitable people. Having a guest is considered an honor—as coming from God. Several times a week I would be invited to a dinner. Usually I lied and said I had work or was busy. I did this because often—not sometimes, but often—in order to serve the guest good meat, and they had to serve meat, a family would spend much of their monthly food budget on this item and then would eat poorly for the rest of the month. So, to avoid guilt, I and the other foreigners were "busy." Of course dinner invitations with people who could afford it were accepted.

Once I was invited to a big dinner at a fairly well-to-do family. They wanted me to bring some friends and said that they were going to surprise me with a special treat. So we went. When the meal was ready, very large old Chinese ceramic plates were brought out covered with food. The largest one had a seeming mountain of pilau, Kabuli Palau, rice with carrots and raisins and nuts and meat hidden inside. It was a huge pile, and my host and friends oohed and ahed about it so much I deduced that the "treat" was special. Since I was the honored guest, I was called out and dutifully came over. They were all snickering and giggling, so I knew I was in for something but good-naturedly took the dish and large spoon I was given. Now I was supposed to dig in and place the pilau on my plate. All the other guests knew what the surprise was and were excitedly watching my every action. So with trepidation, gained through experience, I dug big spoonfuls of rice and carrots out onto my plate, until I hit something solid—the meat! They all cheered. And as I dug away, the vacant eyes of a goat head emerged. All were highly amused at my shocked reaction. In that second, I lost all my appetite. But in politeness, I knew I had to take and to eat all. Gingerly I took off a piece of the forehead and begged off when they offered me other tasty morsels of the head, like the eyes, which, by the way, they kept offering all evening.

# 19

# Saw the River

Every time I went to Herat I passed a particular long stretch of
desert, a soft tan color with those strange jagged, thin mountains. There were few settlements nearby, some flat-roofed
bazaars and domed houses. Houses here were domed because of
the scarcity of wood for beams. Because the sun struck different
areas of the dome during the day, the interiors were remarkably
cool in summer. The thick adobe walls kept it warm in winter. And
being in a domed space is intimate; it gives one a secure, very comforting feeling, very different from the right-angled world most of
us inhabit.

They were the color of the soil they were fashioned from. They appeared totally a part of the terrain. In the changing light of day, the ground and the homes changed from dark, dull brown to bright, glowing gold cut with shadows, which in the angled evening light showed them as bold sculptures—vertical corners, gold on one side, dark on the other, rising to a roof line that bent into a dome, that varied in degrees from light to dark shadows. Simple adobe that in sculptural elegance outshone most attempts at elegance.

Here the two-lane Soviet-built cement highway, strong enough to land planes or to drive tanks on (we were told), crossed a blue river, the Farah Rud, the Farah River.

My eyes always seemed pulled toward these four corners of land bisected by road and water. Later I would learn why.

The Farah Rud flowed south from the huge mass of the Central Mountains visible in the distance. It was a good-sized river for Afghanistan and ran swiftly, blue between dry brown and tan banks of soil and rock. It was undeveloped then.

Scattered mountains stood out to the south, east, and west. They were steep, jagged, some razor-edged, but as you traveled to the side of them, you discovered that the mountains were very thin. It was quite strange, almost like heavy, thick cardboard cut-outs of mountains were scattered here and there like massive, surreal movie sets. Like the mountains in fantastic Persian miniatures.

The river flowed through ruins and areas cultivated off and on for millennia. It was lush until Timur Lenk (Tamerlane) cut the irrigation works in the 1400s, desert and salt since then. Finally reaching the great landlocked depression where Afghanistan, Iran, and Pakistan all meet, the remains of the river form a wetland, a base for hordes of migrating birds, when there is water.

This area, this crossing of road and river, always struck me as unusual and I always felt drawn to it. Later after I got to know Nur and his project with Baluchis, I learned that this was the land they were to settle on. And Nur's land and the piece of land he wanted to give me were in the northeast section of the crossing of the river and the road.

## ❧ 20 ❧

# Students

Several days a week I would go into work an hour early. For this hour I would work teaching English to the men, called *nokars*, workers, or *bachas*, boys. These men were the people who cleaned, ran errands, made and served tea, all the menial jobs. Every office had bachas—and they might be teenagers or *babas* (seniors). I wasn't assigned to teach them, but our manager was a good man and allowed them to learn.

They often lived in a corner of the office or in separate small rooms. Their lives were simple, they were very, very poor, but they often had a great sense of humor which would emerge, provided there was not a boss present who enjoyed power. In these cases, the men trembled when displeasure came. There was one baba in the office, who, as a teen, participated in the revolt of Bacha Saqao (also spelled Bacheh Saqqaw) in 1929. *Saqao* means "water carrier," men who used sewed black goatskins to haul water on their backs to homes, especially to the poor who lived up on the Kabul hills—poor but with wonderful views. The rich lived on the flat land. Miserable work; the damp, cold, heavy skins led to various health problems. Often these men were ethnically Hazara, Shia, who did the backbreaking work of the country, especially in Kabul. *Bacha* in this case meant "son of," *Saqao*, "a water carrier."

In 1928, Pashtun tribesmen revolted against the rule of King Amanollah, who was attempting major reforms of the country based on similar programs in Turkey under Ataturk, and in Iran under Reza Shah Pahlavi. He, and they, believed modernizing reforms were crucial to survival. This was in direct contrast to the Wahhabi seizure of Saudi Arabia, on the one hand, and the colonial rule of the Indian subcontinent by the British, on the other. The king, fiercely opposed to British hegemony in the area, including his kingdom, fought the Third Afghan War in 1919, which, due to British exhaustion in World War I and an airplane bombing Kabul led to quick resolution and full Afghan independence in 1921.

But in 1928, he was overthrown—some say with the connivance of the British and a major conservative Sufi family—and Bacha Saqao, a Tajik bandit hero from the north, took Kabul. His reign of nine months was chaotic. In 1929, the Pashtuns, alarmed by this ethnic Tajik upstart in the capital, rallied around General Nadir Khan, a hero of the recent war, returned from retirement on the Riviera. He was proclaimed king, Nadir Shah. Pashtun rule returned; the country was in their hands again. He ruled for only a few years, assassinated, dying in the arms of his son in 1933. This son, Mohammad Zahir then became king, Zahir Shah.

Back to the office and Baba. He had been an officer in Bacha Saqao's army and was proud of it. Since they had lost, most Bacha Saqao supporters kept quiet, not wanting to provoke anyone's anger. But since Baba was dirt poor and elderly, he said anything he wished about that episode. But when it came to work, he was very careful, very obedient, and above reproach; this meager job with a place to sleep in the closet, was all he had, besides receiving office workers' occasional gifts.

Baba had stories about that war and what had "really" gone on then. And every time he started, within minutes, the gathered people would form into good-natured Pashtun and non-Pashtun camps, and would cheer and boo appropriately.

Well, the Tajiks had this moment of glory in Kabul under Bacha Saqao, and this was repeated in 2001 when the Pashtun-based Taliban collapsed and the Tajik Panjshiri-based Northern Alliance rolled into a liberated Kabul.

Learning from the lessons of history, a Pashtun was quickly found to head the new government—President Karzai. And now another Pashtun group, the Taliban, rule.

Some of my students were also drivers for the vans that carried personnel about town. For high government officials, black Chevrolets were standard then. These students were largely illiterate in their own language and most had never had any schooling. So learning English was hard, filled with ceaseless repeating on their parts after class because they had such difficulty mastering the alphabet and writing things down. But they were enthusiastic, and we all knew that if they could learn enough English to have simple conversations, well then, their position at the office would be secure, they would have increased respect—very important to the senior babas—and best of all they could change jobs, go up in the world and make more desperately needed money.

A year or so after I left this job, I was walking down the street, and a company shuttle van pulled up next to me, and the driver, in a dark uniform, began shouting my name. I couldn't see him well and was confused. Then he came out and greeted me. It was one of my young Hazara students who had obviously moved on, changed jobs. We were both happy to see each other, and he insisted on giving me a ride to where I was going, proudly explaining to the first-irritated, then-amused passengers that I had been his teacher. They all respected and approved his display of courtesy to me, even at their expense and my embarrassment. The understood the value of education.

## ❧ 21 ❧

# Cold

The higher the altitude, the colder the weather. In winter it was very hard to keep warm. Most heaters were like big tin cans with a door, wood-burning. They held no heat, no fire— no warmth. Some heaters were thin metal, conical fireplaces with a grill; you could watch the fire inside. An ingenious device was developed by an American engineer. Instead of burning wood, you patted down sawdust in a metal cylinder and that would slowly burn, much longer than loos sawdust, but sometimes they exploded. In some offices and large old homes, "Russian stoves" were employed. These metal stoves formed part of the wall between two rooms, and heated both. Some were beautifully crafted with hammered copper designs.

A traditional Afghan heater is a *sandolee*, a charcoal brazier which was placed under a low wooden table; quilts were spread over this and people would sit on the floor, lean against pillows, and place their feet under the table with quilts snuggled up to their necks. This system employing electric heaters instead of charcoal is found in many countries, from Japan to Europe.

Walnuts, raisins were considered "warm foods," good for winter.

People would eat, drink tea, play cards, and tell stories. Sadly, because of poor ventilation, sometimes whole families would be found asphyxiated from the charcoal.

Body heat and charcoal. Of course, poor people did with very little. In the high mountains people huddled together under blankets and quilts and slept much of the time. It was almost a hibernation. When these people came to the city to work, they had a hard time staying awake in the winter. During the day, people would squat or sit against the south-facing walls or otherwise try to warm up, soaking in the strong, high-altitude sun, which incidentally was also a helpful sterilizer, useful for food preservation, cleaning used clothes, etc.

Almost all traditional house styles in the country were oriented toward the sun to take advantage of passive solar gain. South-facing rooms had windows with heavy curtains open during the day and drawn shut at night to keep the heat in. Thick walls of adobe or pounded mud, *pise*, held the warmth. And, of course, on floors, cushions and the ever-present wool carpets added to the warmth. And as in old Europe, quilts or rugs or tapestries were hung over doorways to conserve heat, just like the plastic strips in supermarket coolers—these are much better at holding temperature than swinging doors.

Turbans, embroidered skull caps underneath; or wool caps; or Karakul lamb hats or shawls kept the head warm. Shawls were used by women and men, especially in the east and south, draped from the front over the left shoulder, around the neck over the right shoulder; the long end could then be flung around, back over the left shoulder, or the shawl could be draped over the head. Other neighboring countries had different systems, for example, Nepal's system is to throw the end backward over the right shoulder. Throwing the end of one's shawl was done with great grace and sometimes drama, wonderful for an impressive departure. Keeping your head and shoulders covered kept you warm. This is a truth.

On cold winter evenings, I would come home, eat, and sit on a cushion near the conical sheet metal heater where I burned wood to stay warm. It was okay while the fire was burning, though you had to keep water nearby to evaporate because the dry heated air would lead to sinus problems or colds. It was okay while the fire was burning. You could watch it through a grill, but when you went to sleep and it died down, it would quickly become very, very cold. These days there are oil heaters further polluting the air. In winter these wood fires produced a low fog that bathed the streets in a smokey haze. It was oddly dreamlike to walk in this dense smog down streets occasionally lit by a wood fire or car lights, with people gradually becoming visible then slowly disappearing again into the haze.

Sometimes friends who came to dinner would just stay over and we would all sleep in this room. We would sit near the fires, talk, listen to the radio, play music, and talk some more.

One night I was alone; it had clouded over and snow began. Then there was a loud, rumbling in the distance, again and again. Explosions, airplanes? Had the revolution begun? Again, and again, but closer. And then looking through the window, through the clouded sky, I saw flashes of light. Then the light and sounds were more and more coordinated; it was thunder and lightning during a snowstorm. I never knew this could be.

## ❧ 22 ❧

# New Year Picnic Scene

Nauroz (New Year) falls at the spring equinox and has various elements of celebration. People do spring cleaning, get new clothes made, then visit friends and relatives and have *maywah*—a tasty dish of reconstituted dried fruit and nuts. At the end of this two-week period people go out on picnics. One year I accepted the invitation of a friend Yusef, the son of a large Western-educated family, to join them on one. We packed up two Soviet-made Volgas—they reminded me of a 1953 Chevrolet; they looked outdated but they were tough—with food containers and pillows and a big, red Turkoman rug.

Then we headed over the hills north of Kabul to the huge Koh Daman Valley, site of one of Alexander's cities and the now famous Bagram Air Base. The snowcapped Paghman mountains were like a wall on our left, the West. The road followed the base of these mountains. Distant ranges framed the east, and ahead of us was the tremendous white snow-covered wall of the Hindu Kush to the North. The great valley, filed with farms, orchards, vineyards, and villages, was just beginning to green. The air was fresh and the sun nicely warm. Along the mountain slopes we could see where the runoffs from canyons and side valleys were diverted to terraced fields. There were the barren slopes and the line of irrigation channels and the green manmade terraces of farms, like endless steps carved from the lower slopes.

In one of these side valleys you could see the large circular stone drum of what once was a tall Buddhist stupa, Tope Darra. The top was gone and there were cuts in it where robbers had long ago sought hidden treasures. Stupas, found all over the Buddhist world, are solid domed mounds with a relic and often also valuables placed inside. Pilgrims would come and circumambulate as they meditated and prayed. Some said there were two thousand ruined stupas in the country. Most had been broken into at one time or another and most had not been properly archeologically excavated or studied. This was a large one, the circular, careful stonework mostly intact. It sat prominently, high up at the beginning of a small side canyon. It seemed solid and severe even in this state. It has recently been restored to it's basic form but without any Buddhist imagery. Interestingly, Buddhist stupas, even the 90 foot Chakri tower were of stone, and after Islam there was brick and tile.

We drove north until we started to see a pinkish haze to the slopes to our left. It was made up of bushes blooming a solid dark rosy pink. Here and there in the country for various reasons the natural world had been left alone and not cut down or overgrazed. These remnants of what had been were a vivid contrast to the barren desolation, and proof that the land could be very different from what it presently was, if it was allowed simply to be.

We turned left off the two-lane highway and onto a rutted dirt road and followed it up, over rocks and ruts, until we got to a place with wonderful small streams running through the bright green grass and pink-red bushes. It was a paradise! It looked just like the landscapes in traditional Persian miniatures. There were lots of other cars in the area, and people. It was explained to me that this has always been a popular spot, and now with cars more city people were coming. People had thrown rugs down all over the slopes and were sitting, talking, playing music quietly, tending samovars, and eating. It was lively and the bright red rugs electrified the hillsides.

My hosts found a spot to their liking, some distance from the car, and we began to unload our provisions. The mood of all these picnicking families was happy. Many seemed to know one another and exchanged greetings. Yet I found it puzzling. Here were these mostly city people traveling miles to be in nature and then grouping themselves all close together as if there was a need to have safety in numbers, protection from nature, or who knows what. I also noticed that there were no other foreigners around that I could see.

We eventually got all our things out, everyone carried stuff except for the senior men of the family—it would have been improper for them to be seen working—and spread out on the rug. Greetings had been exchanged with neighboring picnickers. We were seated and all set to enjoy our meal. At that point the father noticed a family settling down on a rise not far from us. He suddenly said he would not, could not, stay in such a place near "that family." He got up and rapidly made for the car alone, not carrying anything, careful to avoid "them." The rest of the group was stunned and started to murmur. Next thing I knew we were packing up and carrying everything to the car. Back and forth we went until everything had been retrieved and packed. Of course the father did not help; he was "the man." We got in and drove back to the city. Talk was of the scenery and weather. I dared not ask what had happened, or why. This was not the time. Later, however, I did ask. It turned out that the senior of the other group had slighted the father of my hosts publicly once some years ago. No further attempts at communication were made. It had happened and it was remembered and this remembrance was nurtured.

It was a vivid lesson in the resoluteness with which people acted after their pride had been hurt. There was little talk of forgiveness and examination of one's conscience and personal repentance. Past injustices were not forgotten, and great energy was spent in telling and retelling these episodes. And each retelling was like recharging the battery. The conflict was kept alive, at times for generations, the details carefully enumerated. I recall another family retelling one of these "slights," the teller glossed over some minor point, at once one of the younger members said, "You forgot . . . ." "Oh yes," the teller replied and added it back in—the others nodding in approval, their eyes vague as if they were all busy visualizing the story. A story that had obviously been retold many, many times before. A story that now seemed to be part of every family member's individual personal memory.

Even nowadays I've heard Afghan talk of the days when foreign soldiers were there and how interpreters would ask the soldiers to remove their sunglasses so that tribal elders could see their eyes. The elders knew they were poor and vulnerable but they wanted the soldiers to do this as a simple sign of respect. The elders had nothing else. Also seeing eyes is always a way to "read" another person all over the world. Almost always the soldiers would refuse.

Now after all these years of turmoil, it is even harder to "let go" and "move on." In fact when speaking with Afghans nowadays, such terms are viewed as constructive at times yet also seem to elicit a deep reaction. "Forget it," "Ignore what they did"—that is to be a traitor to one's "own." Pride, family honor, position, and tribal and clan loyalties are the bases of life and security. Nowadays there is great tension between the various ethnic groups.

## ❧ 23 ❧

# Shor Bazaar

S ometimes I would go down to the Shor Bazaar in the old city. It was a bazaar, but not covered. It was basically a narrow pedestrian street that ran parallel to the mountain. Lined with low buildings, it gave way to side alleys and courtyards. Most were very simple adobe buildings, but some were not. They had doorways of intricately carved mellow old wood set into brown adobe walls. Most were not in good condition.

Once inside the court, you looked up and saw balconies and carved glassless windows. They were arched, often with the scalloped arch common to Mughal buildings in India. And the windows had parallel horizontal slats that could be moved or adjusted to allow air circulation or viewing.

The windows were beautifully proportioned, and rows of them brought a sense of great elegance to the adobe-plastered walls. They were old and thus were not greatly valued. Modern was in, old was problematic. But when you entered these old courts, your ties to the present were severed. You were stepping into timelessness. It could be today or one hundred years ago or three hundred years ago or more. The adobe absorbed sound, so it was quiet, and the harsh light refracted against such walls mellowed.

When a person in traditional garb passed through, you really didn't know where or when it was. You could be in a time warp— thrown back hundreds of years. I sometimes had a slight tinge of fear at these times. What if one really had gone back to a time past? What if . . . ? Alone and alien, one would quickly find oneself in challenging situations, and given the country's history, it would be a real challenge to survive.

These old wooden windows and doors were deeply weathered to a mellow brown, which also blended well with the adobe-plastered walls with their embedded, gleaming fragments of chopped, golden straw. These were soothing colors for the eye, a rest from the usually brilliant blue skies and a contrast to the strong colors of traditional dress. And when a door was left ajar, one caught a glimpse of the lush green of a garden and the explosive colors of flowers. All framed within the colors of weathered wood and browned adobe, they seemed psychedelic in intensity.

Somehow I felt free in Shor Bazaar, far from the foreigners and far from the push of modern Afghan society. Yes, I was the tall foreigner, but if I replied to stares with a smile and a greeting, all was well. The people here were poor and very conservative in taste, and they were always polite. There were lots of the usual shops, two to three feet above ground with green or blue or plain wooden shutters, but because of the neighborhood, they sold mostly inexpensive items: matches, cloth, naan. But there were a few holdovers of the old days when this was a major shopping bazaar. It also was a traditional seat of musicians. And many still lived in the area.

My favorite shops were located way down, closer to where the street ended at the rug bazaar. There in an alley to the right they made *rebabs*, a classical Afghan stringed instrument. It has strings you pluck and sympathetic strings that just vibrate when the others are struck. The wooden body, covered in skin, was deep and incised by two semicircular indentations; the neck was usually inlaid with mother-of-pearl. It has a deep, resonating sound and is favored in Kabul and eastern areas and India for classical as well as folk music.

Here the people made rebabs. The shops were small and not elevated above the ground as most were. These were at ground level, with the artisans seated on mats on the bare earth. On the walls were hung tools and partially finished and finished rebabs. On the earthen floor were chunks of wood. The artisans were always gracious and welcoming. They smiled as they worked and answered questions.

That foreigners would come to them or visit a place would bring added respect to it and them. It was publicizing and respecting, and they, like almost all Afghans, didn't just tolerate it, but enjoyed it and treated the visits with great humor. Perhaps because life was at a different pace or perhaps because the culture was so old, people could take even simple occasions or events and make them into enjoyment. They loved wit and loved to point out the absurdity or nonsensicality of things. They could take an incident and work it until some larger story was built up around it, laughing at each exaggeration.

The men used the wood of the *toot*, mulberry tree, to fashion their instruments. The mulberry was an important utilitarian tree.

It grew rapidly and thus its branches could be cut, pollarded, for kindling. In some areas, the leaves were used to feed silkworms, which were then used in local silk production. But most important of all was the fruit, full of vitamins. They had many, many varieties: white, red, black, small, medium, and large. The *shah toot*, king mulberry, was the largest—huge, dark, and dripping with juice. Usually too juicy for market, they were homegrown. In late summer, rooftops were covered with them drying in the sun. After, they would be stored. Sometimes they would be pounded. Dried mulberries were a staple during the winter, especially in the northern mountains.

Here in the bazaar they had good-sized blocks of the yellowish mulberry wood. They would chop and cut and chisel until the desired shapes began to emerge. It was wonderful to look at these deep cut shapes, not simple shapes, not easy or logical, not easy to make, but they were beautiful.

As they carved slowly, the walls would get thinner and thinner until just a shell, the deep body all meticulously dug out. Several of these were always hanging on the walls; aging a bit more before the final stages were begun. I liked these unfinished forms the best— they were sculptures. Solid blocks of wood now rounded, hollow shells of double spheres.

Shor Bazaar and this whole side of the city was bombed to empty shells by the warlord Hekmatyar's troops and others during the Civil War in the 1990s. Tribal rural people, they had little knowledge or respect for the city and history. Often it was viewed as place to plunder similar to their views of India. Large parts of the area were destroyed. Adobe buildings were not fashionable. The modern wealthy Kabuli elites seem to prefer gaudy glass and marble palaces inspired by the worst of Pakistani and Indian modern structures. Later the Agha Khan Trust and the Turquoise Mountain Foundation have helped rebuild and find modern uses for some of these surviving old, beautiful buildings.

# ❧ 24 ❧

# How to Make a Beautiful Tree

Agha once told me how to make a beautiful tree, a tree that would be a centerpiece of a garden, a tree that would live for a long, long time and bring one delight. First you start with a piece of a branch of the willow tree, *majnun*.

You have to do this in the spring when everything is bursting out into life, when the ground is soft and wet and full of moisture. First you have to choose a spot, a special place, a place worthy of the tree's grace.

You start with a branch of *majnun*. This is also the name of a man in a Romeo and Juliet–type story of tragic love, Layla and Majnun. They cannot be together, and so he pines away. The long leaves of the droopy willow branches symbolize the weeping.

You take a piece of a branch about an inch thick, cut off at both ends, about a foot long. You take this piece with its bark intact and pound it into the soft earth—soft so that the bark will not be damaged. You pound it in until only about an inch is above ground level. Then you wait.

Eventually a number of green shoots will begin to grow from the stump. You let them grow for a while and then you cut off all except three, which hopefully are approximately equally spaced apart. You let them grow until they are about a foot long. Then you take these three shoots and gently begin to loosely braid them one over the other just like you braid hair. As the shoots grow, you continue to braid. You can continue doing this for some time, or you can just let it be. Eventually these little shoots will grow out to be the twisted, intertwined brown trunk of a tree that will branch up and over itself and then spread out in hanging branches with long, green, drooping leaves.

These asymmetrical, unusual shapes are highly prized by Afghan gardeners: whether a plant, a tree, or a rock, uniqueness is celebrated. It is beautiful, *maqbul*!

This asymmetry was in great contrast to the geometric layout of the gardens, paths, and orchards. Old Persian miniatures show twisted trees, odd rocks, and irregularity amidst geometric regularity.

*Maqbul!* because, yes, it is beautiful, but also because of the layers of meaning one can "see" if one chooses to. The tragic separation of Majnun from Layla, a common human story, is also taken to symbolize the separation of the soul from "the Beloved," from God.

Thus when you looked at such a tree, you could see the elegant shapes or also you could see Majnun's plight, or also you could see your own.

# ❧ 25 ❧

# Evening Raga

Culturally, Kabul is orientated towards "Hind," the Indian subcontinent. That's where the roads lead, that's where trade is directed, and that's where the movies come from. And then there are the ties of music that are reciprocal, both modern and classical. Afghans played Indian classical and modern music, but they are noted for adding a vibrancy to their performances.

In the north, the ethnic groups gravitated to the larger centers in Central Asia and had their music, Turkmen, Uzbek, Tajik, folk and classical. In the west was the Iranian world. With it's own classical music. In the south and east, it was "Hind" and it's classical and modern music. And everywhere too were the rich layers and variations of local tribal music.

Often, if awake late at night, one could tune in to All India Radio and be transported. During the day they would play classical North Indian ragas. These ragas are very specific. There are pieces appropriate to various times of the day, and to play one at the wrong time is obviously wrong—it sounds off; you just know it is wrong. A piece played at the appropriate time sounds right. My favorites were the ragas for late at night, for midnight and after, especially the vocals.

Summer evenings were for sleeping outside or just sitting, the air cool now with breezes and the sky a dazzling white brilliance of stars. The sound of the city would die off and there was a hushed quiet that only high altitudes can provide. You were relaxed and tired, and then the raga would begin. Slow sounds at first as if reaching out to touch you, but gently, so that you would not be afraid, channels between your own being and the music would gradually open. Slowly the sound would increase; it would be like a plant moving in the wind, or the slow rise of a cobra to the movements of the flute. And then the slow, very deep exhaled syllables would waveringly emerge from deep within the singer. It felt like a great, powerful, giant hand was coming up and under you and immaterially holding you, supporting you, underlying all your shades of being.

The sound was haunting and it echoed and vibrated in sync with the vastness of the Central Asian landscape. It was not necessarily a comforting feeling; it was not soothing. It seductively crept up in you and it seemed to vibrate in the spaces inside yourself. It held you, and you felt held, but it was in a space not part of your known world. It seemed to be a base, a place from which to be taken to other spaces.

Sometimes these night ragas felt like the half moans, not of pain but of waking up to a different dimension, a new arena of experience. The sounds emerging were like you, a person emerging out from one substance, one world, gently into a new . . . a new creation.

The singer, deep, deep into the art, had abandoned the everyday self and in answer to the stirrings, had responded to it by journeying into areas not planned or practiced. They "took off," improvising, creating new sounds as they moved in the void. And as the singer did this, you, too, provided you were attuned, listening, could journey with this new creation, never done before.

You would go off. You knew this for certain, yet could not describe, could not find words for what had happened, what you had learned, what you had experienced. But you had been "someplace."

You would go out, you would feel the journey, you would feel the stretching and the touches and flows that come with learning. But you could not describe what you learned. You could not account for this. You went but knew not where. But you knew that you had been someplace; it was as if you had been drunk, or drugged, or . . . .

And gradually, after all the contortions and frenzy of mind and mood with that raga, then slowly as the music slowed, you would be brought back to your place, a place you began from, and so the raga would end. And it would seem that the raga had spoken of that night, that breeze, that moving branch and all beneath the blazing white band of the Milky Way in the immense dome of heaven.

It had spoken of, encapsulated, a time and space. And by doing this, is had also been a door, a window, a timeless space, a place of no movement, static for all time, yet just a flicker within a moment.

The Taliban feared music and, citing their understanding of the Qur'an, attempted to destroy it. Then they were gone, and people again listened to music, to the ragas, and flocked to the three-hour-long Indian movies from Bollywood. Now the Taliban are back.

## ❧ 26 ❧

# Rugs

Haji was a Turkoman rug merchant with a shop near the end of Jadi Maiwand, the major boulevard that cuts through the old city. This street ended, and on the road to the right and left were the shops of the main rug bazaar, all facing the park-like fairgrounds, where the Taliban later stoned people to death. Haji was a good man, introduced to me by the Sufi family. He'd let people sit in his shop for hours.

He taught customers to feel the wool. Good wool was hard but luxurious, a touch oily. Wool from slaughtered sheep was dry. Nice soft wool wouldn't last in a good rug. And the feel of a really good rug was close to the feel of an animals' pelt. Haji taught you to notice the details in weaving, the extra work on the woven kilim endings of rarer old rugs, the kinds of knots, how to scratch the back of a rug to get an idea of how tightly the knots were tied. It was said that Turkmen women employed opium to help them continue knotting the thousands upon thousands of knots, mostly red, day after day. Some rugs were so tightly woven that the rows of knots literally had to be pounded down into the previous rows. He demonstrated how many folds of a good Turkman can fit in one's hand. Contrary to most ideas, a great Turkman rug is thin, tightly woven, of hard wool, thus the more folds of it in your hand, the more valuable.

It was also important to bend down and breathe on a rug, then to smell. Many new rugs now have a bleach smell. The treatment to the rug softens the wool, makes it look older, increases the sheen, but also weakens and harms the wool. A good Turkoman rug made of top quality hard wool took thirty to fifty years of wear to acquire a beautiful silky sheen, what they termed *bark*, which is actually the Dari word for electricity. A new Pakistani or Indian rug can be made of soft wool but be washed and pressed so much that, brand new, it has this prized sheen. But because of its initial soft wool and brutal treatment, it will not last. Also it is more than likely made by virtual slave child labor—small fingers can make small knots. One of these slave boy rug weavers once ran away and was fortunate to become a symbol of this horror. He traveled, became internationally known, and worked hard to publicize, to stop this abuse, not just in his country. He planned to go to school and become a lawyer. He returned to Pakistan and was quickly assassinated.

Rugs were valued for their bark, and Haji would loan out rugs for a year or so at a time to households that had servants who would sweep the rugs every day, of course mostly with the grain of the rug pile. This would increase the sheen and tighten the knots. The household could enjoy new rugs, and Haji's rugs would increase in value. The sheen too would ensure more contrast when looking at the rug from the direction of the pile (lighter) compared to looking from the end against the pile (much darker). Sometimes it was like looking at two different rugs.

Then too Haji would point out the value of rugs that at first sight looked very uninteresting. They were the usual red with designs in a dull blue or brown, often from the Karakul lambs. These, he emphasized, were made for night by a fire, or by oil lantern or candlelight, or the best, by moonlight. Then these rugs, especially those with a good sheen, would shine and the dull blue would become a soft electric blue color and the dull brown would turn an electric gold hue. And the rugs would bring delight with their shimmering subtleties.

Most rugs were either the brownish or dark colored Baluchi or the red Turkoman rugs—thin with many guls. *Gul* means flower, but in rug designs it refers to small or large repeated medallions. In thin rugs the medallions were small and called guls. In thicker, larger rugs the medallions are large and called *fil poy*—elephant feet. Afghans used certain patterns and rugs were identifiable by tribe and town and design. During the years of war many rug-weaving centers were set up in the refugee camps in Pakistan and people were encouraged to weave according to outsiders' recommendations. This has led to some truly hideous creations, and to rugs no longer identifiable by weave and tribe. Anybody was weaving anything, Afghan, Persian, Turkish, modern, or mixtures. But change also brought good. The Hazaras, not previously weavers, are now producing some of the best rugs. And natural dyes previously mostly supplanted by modern chemical ones have reappeared with beautiful results. Chemical dyes are stable; they don't change or improve with age. Natural dyes change over time, and these changes, combined with increased sheen, result in a rug becoming more attractive and more magical—in a way, a metaphor for how people can age, changing, becoming more attractive and more magical.

During the war, rugs were woven showing battles and weapons—sometimes known as helicopter rugs, for the huge helicopter gunship employed by the Soviets that struck terror into villagers until the arrival of the U.S. stinger missiles. These Stinger Missles, more than the determination or the huge cost of Afghan lives are what ended the war. The prime soviet weapon could be easily shot down with a single shoulder held missile. Technology.

There was a world of discussion, arguments, and positions regarding the interpretation of symbols used in the rugs. But there was general agreement that most meanings were lost, though many seemed to be very similar to designs used in Eastern Europe—a result of ancient Indo-European migrations. In the world of rugs everyone seems to be an expert, and it is strange to be told the names and significance of designs by European or American dealers that are so different from the terms and ideas used in the country of origin.

Rugs woven for dowries are often the finest. And sometimes rugs are woven by commission. They are investments; when one needs money, one can always sell, and of course a good rug always appreciates in value. And in the meantime they cover the floors, and keep you warmer in winter, and, spread on the ground, make a picnic more special. Raised platforms of pounded earth or of carved wood in a garden are covered with them. And when, moving from the drab brown fields and streets, one enters a high adobe walled garden, the sight of red rugs and cushions set amidst a world of flowers and green trees brings one into a world of no time or thoughts but only an almost meditative awareness of the present.

## ❧ 27 ❧

# Malang in the Hindu Kush

There was a man who lived on the northern slopes of the Hindu Kush. This massive mountain range bisected the country from the northeast tapering down towards the southwest. It is part of the humongous swirl of mountain ranges that sort of spin out of the knot of the Karakorums. The Himalayas swirl to the east, the Hindu Kush to the west, and the Tien Shan to the north. The very name *Hindu*

*Kush* translates as "Hindu Killer." Supposedly this refers to the time several thousand years ago when the Hindus, one branch of the Aryans who also settled Iran and Europe, migrated from Central Asia. They crossed the mountains, Hindu Kush, where many died, and continued south—taking control of Afghanistan, Pakistan, and northern India, driving the indigenous darker-skinned peoples to the hills, the deserts, or to southern India. Others said the name came from the intense cold and how the Hindu merchants from warm "Hind" would perish attempting to cross the high passes. The south-facing slopes were fairly barren; the northern ones had forests of scattered trees and running trout streams. This is because the moisture-bearing clouds from the north drop their rains here when they hit this huge wall.

To cross the mountains you would drive north from Kabul, through the vast Koh Daman Valley, then up and up the narrow

Salang Valley, past unwalled stone Tajik villages built on stone terraces. In the south and east the Pastuns lived in fort-liked walled compounds. This reflected the vast cultural differences in the country. Orchards and fields beautifully descended in huge steps cut into the massive slopes. Higher up, the farms gave way to barren slopes with occasional streams. The two-lane road twisted up the valley to the entrance to the Soviet built Salang Tunnel at 11,200 feet. The mountains still loomed up, way above.

People said that the mountains were so high that some birds could not fly over them. They had to land and walk over the ridges. And they said that people from the valleys would hike up and set up large nets on the ground to catch them as they walked over. Birds, no matter how small, were deemed tasty treats.

The Salang Tunnel was narrow, dark, cold, and driving through it was always unsettling. We once stopped to admire the view at the south end. There was a taxi half buried in the snowdrift. The people said they had lost their brakes coming through the tunnel. They were fortunate to have driven into the snow bank. The rest of the turn had only a steep drop of thousands of feet. When the tunnel opened up on the northern side, you were in a different world. The road snaked down, but there was much more vegetation, trees!, and there were many more streams, greenish from the glacial run-offs. Evaporation is always slower on shaded northern slopes, so the snows melt slower and the water can sink in and nurture growth.

You looked down and the ridges and mountains grew lower and lower, and you knew that it all ended in the vast Eurasian plains that stretched all the way to central Europe. Here and there on the road were teahouses: usually a simple adobe and wood structure, next to a stream, with raised wood platforms in front covered with red rugs where travelers could stop, sit, recline, drink a pot of tea, have a simple meal in the warm sunlight, surrounded by the sound of rushing water. On one of the platforms would sit one of the huge, old, barrel-shaped, gold-colored brass Russian samovars, about three feet tall. These were everywhere in the country and some dated from czarist Russian times. From the city of Tula, Russia, they were made to last.

They simply boiled water. Burning charcoal was placed in the chimney core that ran through the center of the drum, and so the water in the surrounding drum would be heated. When lit, they spewed aromatic smoke, sometimes sputtered and shook, and seemed to be creatures from some animated cartoon. Anyone will tell you that tea brewed from water from a real samovar has a much superior taste. A large spout with a stylized animal head on the spigot allowed water to be poured into teapots containing black or green tea leaves. The pot would be served to you with a handle-less cup. Sugar or hard candy was always available to sweeten the brew. The piece of hard sugar or candy was placed between one's teeth and the tea came through sweetened.

Sometimes a carpeted wooden platform would span the stream and you could drink, sit relaxing inches above the cold, clear water. The scent of burning wood fires, the taste of hot tea held in your hands in a sometimes very old ceramic bowl, seated on a bold red rug inches above the rush of a glacial stream surrounded by green grass and flowers and cedar forests and snow-covered peaks—they would say *behesht*, paradise! Afghans understood the joys of the simple in a very Japanese way. Sitting with flowers or on a red rug inches from water was better than just looking.

Several times, while taking this route, I saw a man out alone, walking the ridges. Once or twice I saw him up close. He was not dressed in the usual, pajama-like, perani tombans but had a kind of ragged and torn robe and hat and long, black hair. He was robust-looking, not thin, and seemed possessed of an amazing amount of energy. His eyes were clear and forceful. He was a *malang*, a person who dedicated his life to spiritual development; he sought to touch the God by following this way.

The stories were that he lived alone, was highly educated, never asked for food or help, walked barefoot even in the deep snows with no other clothing than what he wore. He was a free person. You got that sense just watching him. Sometimes he would come to the teahouses to talk with people about God, but would never accept anything from them. He was amazing to watch, energetic, happy, and free in his mountains.

People like him were treated with respect. Some said a malang might be a crazy person or a holy person, crazy with the God. Who could tell—so we must treat them well and respect them. I wonder where the malangs are in our modern world. If we look, we probably will see people touched by an alternate reality who are having a marginal life in our society, perhaps medicated.

# Nur and Agriculture

Nur Agha was very interested in agriculture and was constantly trying new ways to improve the family farm. On the farm there were a few walled gardens that had date groves. When his grandfather had fled the Middle East, actually they were part of a large Sufi family in Baghdad, but this part of he family had been exiled by the then British overlords for political activity. They went east to Afghanistan. Here, given land by the king he had planted these groves, supposedly the only ones in the country. They were lush dark green, and they covered everything in deep shade. Other gardens had citrus fruit and vegetables, and then there were fields of rice and wheat. Besides his interest in new agricultural developments, in increased yield and income, he also was keenly interested in getting the local farmers involved in new crops and technologies. He wanted everyone to "go up."

There were some government agricultural advisors who were well trained and who were involved in projects with foreign "experts." But the farmers were suspicious. Sometimes advisors, both foreign and local, had good intentions and projects, but sometimes they lacked familiarity with local microclimates. Over generations many areas had developed their own strains of wheat and rice, based on their specific climatic and water constraints. An advisor might come in with glowing reports of a new hybrid, and farmers might try it only to see it fail, due to some unique local conditions. Or the government might urge some new project only to drop it due to a shortage of funds or a change in political priorities or whatever. So they listened to outsiders but moved slowly. Now Nur Agha told me that if he, a trusted religious leader, tried something new, well, then the farmers would be much more open to something new.

# ⊗ 29 ⊗

# Crown the Taj

I had come back from my first trip to India. Though I had not traveled far, I saw a lot in the Delhi–Agra area. I was overwhelmed by strong and conflicting impressions—the sophistication in art and architecture, music, food, clothes, the desperate, numbing poverty, the incredible, rich layers of cultures, the blank hungry stares of the poor.

I went to visit Agha and he asked me many questions about my experiences. Then he asked me what had struck me the hardest, what had impressed me the most. My answer was crystal clear to me: the Taj Mahal—the tomb built from 1631 to 1653 by the Mughal Emperor Shah Jahan (King of the World) for his beloved wife, Mumtaz Mahal (Chosen One of the Palace). It is a sculpture of his love for her, a masterpiece of white Indian marble that blended Persian and Hindu forms and workmanship into a sophistication of art and form and proportion rarely seen. It is the best of India—a CREATION—a mixing and blending of forms, traditions, and religions to produce something new, a synthesis, the next step up, a cutting edge, onto a higher plane.

It is set at the end of a large, walled garden. At the opposite side a central gate faces it with long pools of water leading up to it, and pools crosswise divide the garden into four quarters, with a small elevated pool and a single bench in the center.

The Taj itself is built on a raised platform with minarets in the four corners leaning slightly outward. In case of earthquakes they will fall away from the building. They are locked. Too many broken-hearted lovers had used these 120-foot towers to end their sufferings. To balance and frame this huge, white structure, a red sandstone mosque was built on one side and a matching building was placed on the other side—just for balance. Behind this was space; the terrace broke off abruptly to the River Yamuna below. Across the river were the walls of a matching garden where Shah Jahan supposedly planned a matching black marble tomb for himself.

I told him that I saw the Taj first from the tower of the Itimad ud Daulah, an earlier tomb that first utilized inlaid colored stone, instead of the Persian mosaic glazed-tile techniques, to form designs. It is like a jewelry box with short minarets, upriver from the Taj. At my first view of the Taj from the top of this tower I thought, "Oh, it's a Hollywood movie set," the way it glowed in the distance—huge and white. Then with a jolt, I realized I was not looking at a movie, it was not a prop. It was it!

I had seen its shape repeatedly by the time I finally approached its red sandstone garden walls. I climbed the steps of the gatehouse and entered the dark hall that led to the inner garden. From the darkness, the view into the garden was framed by a huge, pointed Persian archway, similar to an English Tudor arch. As my eyes adjusted to the dim light, I began to see what looked like a gleaming white illusion far beyond the arch. I froze and just stared at this unearthly beauty.

I remember people pushing past me, irritated that I was blocking their way. Gradually, I realized this and moved forward. Once outside, I quickly moved to the left and sat on a red sandstone ledge and I cried. I recall that only one simple idea kept coming through my mind and tears, "Beauty can transform, beauty can transform."

Later I thought of how people often live in ugly, violent environments, and not just the poor. If only there were more beauty in their lives—then the violence might decrease, the rat race would ease, or at least the beauty would soften their existence. Or perhaps rich or poor people, everyone, should make beauty, should fashion it somehow with their own hands, in their own ways.

I recalled old friends who told me of the Ukrainian tale about why they made *pysanke*, now called Easter eggs. Intricately decorated eggs taking hours of wax batik work, for what? On a very breakable eggshell! Well, there is a monster, Evil, chained to a great mountain. The more pysanke, the more beauty is created in the world, the more secure the chains. But if there is less beauty created, then the monster, Evil, will spread throughout the world. So thus it is up to each person, each of us, to make beauty, to limit the spread of evil.

The Taj, huge and spellbinding, is a sculpture. I saw it in the morning, in the afternoon. And it was different. At the time of my first visit, India and Pakistan were involved in one of their brotherly wars. And you could see rooms filled with stacks of camouflage netting through the grills on doors in the terrace supporting the building. The building was actually covered with netting during wartime. The marble glowed at night and Pakistani pilots, who would absolutely never harm the building, would use it as a beacon to locate a nearby modern petroleum complex, whose fumes were actually eroding the marble structure.

The Lords of Renaissance Florence sponsored the revival of the ancient Roman technique of Pietra Dura, stone inlayed into stone to create pictures and designs. Semi-precious stones were used. Light hitting this surface did not act like it did on flat surfaces like paintings. No, the light penetrated into some stones and bounced back. At times it glowed. Some of these Florentine inlaid plaques came to the Moghuls. One is imbedded above the throne in the

Red Fort in Delhi. The Moghuls appreciated the jewel like surfaces and adopted this art form in an Indian manner. And so the white marble of the Taj is inlaid with stones and semi-precious stones in floral designs and calligraphy. And one can see the carnelians used in orange red flowers.

In those days, the garden was open during the nights of the full moon. I should explain that tombs and cemeteries in many countries are not gloomy sites, but places for picnics and visits. Living, dying was all natural. This was an old tradition of the Taj. In the nights of the full moon, the building glowed more than usual; it shimmered, and the shades of color changed white to pink to purple to blue, to colors I don't know the name of.

And far away, from the garden, you could see through the open doorway, the light of the single lamp, hanging from the dome, above the tombs. Only one light, that was all, a gift of Lord Curzon who was responsible for its rehabilitation.

One night as I was wandering in the moonlit halls, I heard beautiful flute music echoing through the stone walls. I found him. The man was sitting in a side building against a pillar, looking at the Taj and playing. Later I spoke with him; he did not want money. He was just spending the night, reading love poetry about the beloved and separation, and playing and praying. "The beloved" could be one's love or God.

I told Agha all about this. He nodded, as was his way. And at the end, he asked me who built the Taj. I said, "Shah Jahan."

"Yes, but who was he?"

"Emperor of the Mughals." (A form of the word *Mongol*. Yes, they were descendants of the Mongols.)

"Would you like to live under his rule?"

"Absolutely not," I said. "After years in the country, I appreciate the horrors of being subject to another's arbitrary rule. I much prefer my rights under a democracy." "A democracy," he said.

"Yes," I said.

"Yet you like the Taj?"

"Of course!"

"But who built it?"

I said that I didn't get it.

"Well," he said, "the Taj was built by an emperor. It took the resources of an empire to design and construct it. But it is there and will be there for many centuries to come. You have your democracy and your tremendous wealth, but could your society build anything like that—a building 'to love'?"

"No, I don't think we could."

He then asked, "Which do you prefer, a supreme example of human ability like the Taj Mahal, or democracy?"

It was not so simple, I thought. Yet in some ways, it was. We did not and we have not.

"Your system cannot build a Taj," he said. The old system, based on family and full of corruption and such problems, could build Taj Mahals to bring beauty and to teach and inspire, to stir the hurt, to reawaken pieces of the soul and to stimulate and urge people to actions.

Later, I thought too of, say, Renaissance Italy, where families and the church vied with each other to have art glorify their names. Great art and science were created. Yet in our age, despite the staggering wealth of some individuals and families and of some nations, there is not great patronage of building, of the arts, of creating "new" beauty. The great tech lords of California and elsewhere are not acting like the lords of the Renaissance, or the lords of all the old cultures of the world, India, China, Japan, Europe, . . . A little goes in this direction, but mostly the money seems to go to support elite lifestyles and more tech. There is little giving back to the country, to the culture, to the people who have paid for the foundations of this world and have supported these Tech developments. The quality of life is ignored. Beauty is not fed. They build no Taj, or public beauty.

Few artists or artisans have generous patrons. Few cities are blessed with inspired, sponsored public art. The art world has become a business. It is often clever, intellectual, conceptual. But does it move one as the great art of any culture does?

Agha had a good point, and as always, a lesson.

## ❧ 30 ☙

# In March

"When will you visit me in Jalalabad?" Nur Agha asked.

"I don't know; in March sometime."

In winter, Afghans moved if they could, or sent family down to this subtropical area on the way to the Khyber Pass, the pass to Pakistan and India. Oranges grew there; every year poets went there to a convention when the orange blossoms perfumed the air. It's surrounded by snowcapped mountains. Forested Nuristan is to the north and Tora Bora, of Ben Laden fame, to the south.

One Friday I left my house to go to the taxi *saroi*, station, to share a ride to Jalalabad. But on the way I ran into friends from the provinces who needed a place to stay, so I changed my plans and stayed in town.

The next week I went down to his farm, got out of the taxi, and walked the miles down a side dirt road. Near the farm, I recognized one of his workers squatting by the side of the road. He waved me over, greeted me, and led me through green fields to a walled garden away from Nur Agha's walled compound. Inside I saw peacocks, a magnificent horse, and a group of men further down the raised orchard paths; he was with them. We greeted each other and he showed me around. With him was a group including a man in spectacles with a large hawk on his shoulder. Nur explained that the bird would hunt our lunch for us.

Later in the visit I asked Nur Agha why his workman was there, expecting me by the side of the road. "Oh, I saw you coming last night in a dream so I sent him out at about the time I felt you would arrive." I was still digesting this when he added, "But I saw you coming last week and almost sent someone to meet you, but then felt I shouldn't. Were you coming?" I answered that I was but that guests had changed my plans. His comments then seemed normal to me, just part of our relationship. But most people would doubt.

In Kabul his room was very spare: place to sit, bed, bookcases, desk with two glass candlesticks with glass globes. I asked once what they were for. He said at night he stays up and does exercises with the lights to increase his abilities.

# ৩১ ৯

# Heratis and Their Trees

There were twenty thousand huge pine trees in the city, planted hundreds of years ago, until 1885. At that time the Afghans were defending the city from a Persian attack. The defenders decided that the madrassahs at the Musical Complex by Gawhar Shad's tomb had to be leveled since guns could be placed on them to fire into the city. Also since the trees could burn, they had to be leveled. This was all done, the Persians were defeated, and Herat stayed in Afghanistan. But the trees were gone and the city went into official mourning for years. Their beloved huge trees were gone. Some were planted but it was not until the 1940s that an enlightened governor replanted and lined the roads coming into the city for twenty kilometers with thirty two thousand trees. Yes, to provide shade and beauty but also to restore some of their old pride. Now of course, the trees again fell during the recent wars, for winter and cooking fuel. Photos show bleak scenes. Now they are replanting again.

The huge great Masjid-e Juma, Friday Mosque, had eleventh-century remnants but was mostly Timurid. Some old ceramic tiles remained on the walls, but most was whitewashed. Old photos show this along with the deep sculptural qualities of the court-yard structure. Large, open *iwans*, vaulted spaces open on one side opening onto the middle of each side of the square central court. All was white.

In the 1920s the people decided to place a voluntary tax on sugar. The proceeds would be used to gradually retile the structure. The deep blues of the Timurid work has given way to more vibrantly colored Afghan designs. And the workshop still continues its work, breaking solid, colored tiles into pieces that are cut and fitted together as mosaics. The face-down designs are covered with cement, making panels that are then lifted up and set into the walls, with cement sides in and with the tiles facing out. Other panels are made by painting designs across flat tiles, which are then fired. But the mosaic work, costly, is ever changing in daylight, or dark and wondrous.

Now the designs themselves are remnants of the old world. A projector slide of one design will reveal various different designs embedded in a pattern when the focus is changed. It is said that the designs are based on the old Hindu number grid. Our Western number system is called the Arabic system, but it was conveyed to Europe via Arab or Muslim traders who in turn got it from India, where it had been developed by the theoretically minded higher castes.

So, take a grid, nine squares across and nine squares down, with numerals 1 through 9 going across left to right, and 1 through 9 top to bottom along the left side. Then, following these coordinates on this grid, one fills in the square. For example a 3 across, a 2 down: 3x2 brings a 6 into its square, but a 6 across and a 2 down produces a 12, which is reduced to a 1+2=3, so 3 is placed in the square. The grid is filled. Then a number, say, 2, is chosen and isolated from the others, all the 2s are connected by lines, and a design emerges, geometric, or a floral one can be developed. Different concepts or ideas are assigned to each number. Thus panels can be read: say, a 2 is education, which leads to a 3, which is experience; these two numerals lead to, say, a 4, which is understanding. One concept can lead to another. You can let your mind go, following lines to flowers to stars within lines. The mazes lead to being amazed, and leading to other and deeper realities.

This is what they are made for. One is supposed to "let go," lose oneself in order to expand, an ironic contradiction. But very few these days even know about the grid or the Sufi concepts said to be embedded in this skeleton for the design.

One day I was outside beside the mosque and suddenly heard loud, sharp sounds like a boom, or screams all at once—or large drums, my rational mind countered. It didn't make sense that it came from the mosque, dogs are "haram" forbidden, dirty, yet it seemed to. Absolutely no dogs there, nor drums. It had a raw, very powerful energy. Yet, it didn't feel "not safe." Curiosity drew me. It grew louder as I walked down the dark, vaulted passageway that led to the sun-filled courtyard. The sound was very loud now and almost urgent. I stepped into the light and froze. To the right, in front of a large, marble *mihrab*, which indicates the direction of Mecca and that stood alone in the courtyard, was a circle of men facing inward, standing then bowing deeply, exhaling what sounded like "hoo" loudly, upright, then bowing, then upright, over and over. The bows were deep, from the waist, then upright:

"Hoo, Hoo, Hoo." Turbans flew off, some heads were traditionally shaved, others surprisingly had long hair, which now flew into and out of the circle. In the center was a man with a taller turban who calmly faced each and then moved on to the next. He seemed to be making sure that they were coordinated. Outside the circle were others seated on the flat brick pavement and one man standing who sang—not in sync with them, but independently of the booming chant.

His song was light, beautiful, as a small bird flying above this heaving mass. I was quite a distance from them and moved to a vaulted area to be less obtrusive. They were hyperventilating; starting from a slow beat they moved to a rapid beat and finally slowed again. At another time I brought friends along to see this ceremony, the *zikr*. My friends left because we all started to breathe in time to the chant; it was that compelling, that forceful. At other times, I watched through a large keyhole-shaped arched doorway. Men in one group, women veiled, but not all in *chador*, sitting in a circle nearby. Another time in a glassed-in iwan that faced south—warm in the winter—I sat with others, leaning against a wall while the circle chanted. There was an elderly man with a large metal cane sitting near—no one special, I thought. He nodded welcome. The circle seemed open to all. Several individuals were clearly psychologically disturbed yet were allowed to join as long as they stayed coordinated with the rest. As the chanting slowed, the man with the cane began to chant and changed the focus, again and again, slower, faster, lighter, more intense. He clearly was a leader. When it was over, as we left, he called me to him and pointed to his cheek for me to kiss. Later in the bazaar, buying melon seeds, a merchant also pointed to his cheek and I kissed his cheek. He too had been there.

These people were all Sufis. Sufis came in all packages—liberal, conservative, loving, dangerous. They have teachers and seek deeper truth and understanding—some use music, or breathing exercises, or whirling, or calligraphy, or meditations, or art or other avenues to go to deeper levels of consciousness. Different groups have different views, and that means you go to the one that fits your personal construction best. Dervishes are Sufis, only full-time.

On one summer evening, two friends and I were walking in the Great Friday Mosque. It was still light when we entered. The colored tile sheathed the courtyard surfaces with a skin of various designs, and the dimming light altered the designs—they all kept changing. Sometimes the irregular surfaces of the mosaic panels shot back pieces of light, sometimes just a glimmer. Some panels reflected no colors but only the patterns of the broken pieces, different pieces of light fitted together, each part a different sheen. The painted tile panels were muted by their one-dimensional surface. The iwans and archways framed shadowed areas that receded into deeper darkness.

The white inner vaults were now some color I don't know the name of. It wasn't white anymore, but I don't know what it was. It was quiet; only a few people were seen passing through or sitting in some silent prayer or contemplation. I remember the sky being that strange, almost neon but quiet, deep light blue that only desert air can provide. Venus appeared, then other stars and there was just the silver sliver of a classical Islamic crescent moon to the left above the iwan, the vault, facing Mecca.

We walked by an elderly gentleman who greeted us. We responded with the appropriate Afghan courtesy responses and a conversation ensued. He inquired as to our countries and occupations. We answered and took him to be a simple gentleman, the kind you often found in the country, polite, friendly, with a dignified bearing. Generally not highly educated by our standards yet often possessing an astonishing knowledge and memory of classical Persian poetry along with understanding of its depths and concepts. We often found people who were aware of outside world developments but put their own stamp of understanding on the events. So we asked him if he believed that man had reached the moon and had walked on it. He looked at each of us in turn and said, yes, indeed they had gone there. We all then commented on how strange it seemed to be looking at that far crescent and to picture humans up there.

Yes, he said, people have gone to the moon. Yes, and he pointed at us, you can go to the moon or to Mars or Jupiter or even Pluto, he said, or to another galaxy. At this point I think we realized that we were not just speaking with an elderly gentleman. You can go, he said, but you have not gone anywhere until you have gone here, and he pointed to his chest. You have not gone anywhere unless you have gone inside yourself. Unless you have gone there, started that endless inner journey, all the traveling one has done, the people met, all the things one has learned and experienced doing so, all the money one has made, amounts to nothing. With our limited understanding we agreed, spoke more, and eventually went our way, troubled yet pleased by the encounter. A few days later we related this incident to a Herati and described the man to him. He was impressed at our good fortune and stated that the man was the head of the mosque.

Once I was standing on the top of some ruins and looked around, north, at the views. Just below were the black tents and camp of some nomadic families. A man came out and called me over—I went down. He said that a teenage relative of his with no family was very ill. He had brought her to the hospital in the city but was unable to pay the bribe to get her admitted. He also said that he didn't have any money to pay for medication even if they had accepted her. He insisted that I see her and asked, "What should I do?" He opened the flap of the tent and I saw her leaning against some bags. Very thin, her skin was pale, alabaster-like, with the quiet translucent glow some sick people develop.

There was an unearthly beauty about her. I felt that she was dying. I would give him some money for her but doubted whether she would benefit from it. Perhaps he would spend it on getting her admitted to a hospital or perhaps he would spend it on his own poor family, or perhaps it was all a begging scam. All this flooded my head as I climbed back up the slope. On top were healthy-looking people and an army officer with his family.

I usually stayed away from the military, but the officer asked what I had been doing with the nomads, and I explained the situation and my dilemma. (I should explain that the Afghan government had once asked President Eisenhower for American training for their armed forces. Eisenhower, always warning of the military industrial complex, declined, so the Soviets trained the army. Many thought this was a terrible idea.) The officer became angry and shouted, "These people need discipline. There is no discipline in this country. Soon we will have changes in this country and we will have discipline!" I remember turning cold, feeling deeply cold deep inside myself, given what I knew of Soviet history and its artificial famines and purges, and the ideology of the Afghan army being Soviet-inclined.

For them, simple people were not important in the grand, "correct" picture of a world ideology. Ironically the Taliban and related groups have an identical mentality. We are nothing in the big picture; *world peace* meant, means, "under their rule", be it communist or the "salaam" of the radical Islamicists. The beggars and the dying, the military, and the dialogue—I left upset, feeling I had experienced something much bigger than what I had seen. This was before the war.

Later, during the time of chaos, conflicting reports emerged from the city. One story went this way—the people revolted against the Soviet installed regime and took over the city. A group of

Soviet "experts" were captured and eventually

skinned alive. In retaliation, the Soviet planes bombed the city, sort of a foretaste of Grozny, Chechnya. It was said that twenty thousand women and children took sanctuary in the great Friday Mosque—it was bombed and they were slaughtered, the mosque destroyed.

Nowadays, Herat has peace, parks, and its own university. However, women and opponents have great problems. The Friday Mosque still stands. But due to the various bombardments, the blue glazed tiles have fallen off Gawhar Shad's ribbed dome mausoleum.

And the minarets, most still standing, have shed their marble and tile coverings—now just brown brick, industrial-looking towers. And the vast adobe maze of the city in brown earth with green trees in gardens is now punctured by glass and marble, modern palaces built by the moneyed. Iranian money pours in to their Shia brethren, but most Heratis remain Heratis.

## ❧ 32 ❧

# Coup Night

It was summer. Days hot, nights cool, pleasant. The king was in Italy, someone said, visiting one of his girlfriends. It is the practical custom in this part of the world to sleep on your roof or in your garden or courtyard during the summer. The cooler night air, the freshness, the freedom from walls and the stuffiness of rooms, a chance to look up at the stars under the great dome of heaven are the reasons given.

It is also a touch back to many people's nomadic past.

We set up *charpoyees*, bed frames made of poles, strung with rope, covered by cotton cushions and sheets or thin blankets in the garden. It was a clear night, warm and pleasant.

Deep in the night we were suddenly awakened by some explosions and gunfire. Shots at night were not that uncommon—could be a wedding celebration, or a feud, or . . . . But it all continued, coming from the direction of central Kabul and the palace. Then the sound of a helicopter neared. We peered over the walls, saw deserted streets, and then saw it approaching, low over the houses, with its spotlight illuminating the ground below. It was coming our way. We grew alarmed. The house was at the bottom of a low hill, at the top of which was a military fort, a *qala*. It was timeless, low, massive, almost oval in shape, thick adobe walls with a single pronounced arched gateway. It was occupied by the military, so you never ventured too close.

But the story went that in the earlier part of the century, nitroglycerin was brought here and stored and more or less forgotten. It had been there so long that it had solidified, according to one story, or at least was in a less stable state. Supposedly foreign experts had been brought in but no one could suggest a practical way to remove the material. So everyone knew that there was a large amount of unstable explosives stored there. Now amidst the firing, a helicopter was approaching the fort, the qala.

Stories raced through my mind. Since we had arrived, Afghans had spoken of a coming revolution, of a need to change the order of things. This was not just from the city dwellers but also from rural farmers and nomadic people. But, then, Afghans liked to tell stories, so you wondered how deep this urge for change was—because they also had stories about past fighting and revolts, and they deeply feared the violence.

Many loved the story about how, in 1842 during the first AngloAfghan War, British, Indians, and staff evacuated Kabul, but only one Englishman reached the British lines. The rest—seventeen thousand, mostly Indians—were killed, captured. The women were captured, kept in the caves at Bamiyan and returned, unharmed. The British had negotiated a surrender of arms where they would withdraw but the Afghan government side did not provide protection from the tribes. They were slaughtered. The British were led by general Elpinstone probably the most incompetent general in British History. He reportedly had a dozen horses used just to carry his dinnerware. In my time there was talk of evacuation in case of revolution, but even this concept was full of problems in light of reality. To the west, it was hundreds of miles to Iran; north meant crossing the Hindu Kush Mountains and facing a then-unknown Soviet reception; south was desert until you reached the Arabian Sea, far away. The only way out to safety was to Pakistan, either via the pass the British had used or via the modern road through a narrow, deep gorge, or other rough trails, all of which went through tribal territory, a place of no government and of individual tribal policies and whim.

We had not been informed of any American evacuation plan, in case of emergencies like this, so we stayed in our compound. The helicopter kept coming, louder and louder, and we heard a few gunshots, coming from the Fort. Roaring, it slowly flew low, directly over us. The garden, everything, was illuminated by the bright light. It was like being in a Persian miniature—everything was flood lit and bold. The greens were super green, each flower stood out like a small explosion of color. It was very surreal to be bathed in that light.

Almost blinding, it was like being a deer caught in a car's headlights. You were stunned, yes, by the light, but much of it was just that you were shocked, fascinated, almost hypnotized by this stark illumination of things you thought you knew. You knew what a leaf looked like but now, no, a leaf was now so much more. Surreal too in not knowing, and wondering if fighting was going to break out a few hundred feet from us. And if it did, what would happen to the explosives? Would we and the whole hill go up in a cloud of dust? The helicopter circled and illuminated the Fort with its lights. The fort seemed larger than usual, closer, and details stood out. The air was filled with the sound of the engines and blades and with booms and machine gunfire and shots from a distance.

The copter landed by the gateway, still roaring; no shots were heard and later it left. Relieved by the end of our immediate danger, we now focused on the fighting. It lasted sporadically the rest of the night but it was not from everywhere; by morning, only from one area, the Royal Dilkusha Palace, the "heart's delight palace."

From over the walls, we saw people gradually emerging from their houses, but traffic was sparse. Walking down the street, I coldly observed tanks at major intersections but groups of people nearby suggested all was well. As I got closer, I saw the tanks covered with flowers, garlands hanging from the gun turrets.

People stared at the few dead bodies left in the streets as they gradually went about their daily business. Authoritarian Daud Khan, the king's cousin, former tough prime minister, was now in control with his Soviet-trained army. His picture was now rapidly replacing the king's in all the shops. People said the air force and some generals were still loyal to the king. So there still might be more serious fighting. Also, the shah of Iran had reportedly offered his help in restoring the monarchy. But the king was in sunny Italy, some said, on the beautiful island of Ischia with his girlfriends. Supposedly wanting to spare bloodshed, he abdicated.

The queen, on the other hand, was still in the palace, holed up with the royal guard, refusing to surrender. She held up for days, negotiating, some said, to be allowed to leave with her jewelry.

Zahir Shah's father, Nadir Shah, had been assassinated in front of him by a student at a school graduation, just a few years into his reign in 1933. To his credit, the boy prevented the guards from massacring all the students on the spot. He was placed on the throne, young, but his father's brothers, his uncles, controlled and dominated.

They were renowned for their toughness and cruelty. There are many stories of how they used their power, forced whole tribes to move, on and on. Individual stories were also common, such as the owner of a bread shop who, accused of overcharging, was thrown into his tandoori oven. According to the stories, Zahir Shah's uncles tried to toughen up the boy king, to make a man out of him, subjecting him to their cruelty and whims. Perhaps this all led to the later indecision in his reign and his abdication and remoteness during the country's twenty years of agony in war. During that time, he lived in Italy and said and did almost nothing about the war, about the ten million refugees, about the hunger. He never asked or begged the world for help for these people, as Haile Selassie of Ethiopia did before the World when Italy's Mussolini mercilessly invaded his country. Some people later condemned the king for this, mostly the non-Pashtuns. But many Afghans, mostly Pashtun, who supported him never criticized him for this—he was the king, a Pashtun, to be respected; he was a cultural elder, not to be questioned. One does not tell what others call "the truth" to one's elders in the family, to those in power, especially to the country's leader.

# ⊰ 33 ⊱

# Perceptions

Abdullah, hired to do basic chores around the house, brought his brother, Ali, to work to teach him, to train him to be a "servant." He was straight down from the Hazarajat, the mountainous homeland of the Hazara people, and eager to learn. One day he came to me with his hand closed and told me to open it—I did. There was a live scorpion inside. He laughed. And went away playing with it.

One day Abdul told Ali to sweep and wipe the windows in the common room. At that time I was trying to promote the work of a painter of miniatures and had a few simple samples on wood lined up on a shelf. After work that evening I noticed that several of them were badly smudged. I asked Abdul about this. He in turn said it was Ali's responsibility. Ali answered that he had wiped the boards with a moist cloth. Why? I asked, couldn't he see that they were pictures? No, he said. I tested him and asked what he saw on the other boards—he had a difficult time identifying the figures in them. Abdul had never had any schooling; he came from a very remote area, and had not had much exposure. When he focused and was told to look carefully, he did see the pictures. He simply needed information.

One day I showed a movie about American life to the staff where I worked. It was a very fast-paced film made up of short vignettes. Afterwards they all said they liked it and many wanted to see it

145

again. But when I asked about what they had seen, most said they saw lots of pretty colors—only a few identified people and actions. I was surprised and so we explored their reactions. They simply were not used to perceiving rapidly changing images.

The stories went that rural people new to cities had a hard time crossing traffic. They would freeze, get hit, or run the wrong way. People theorized that when they saw a car or truck coming, they gauged its speed according to those speeds they were familiar with, those of a horse, donkey, or man. It was perfectly reasonable. Their system saw a car but they assumed that it moved at the pace of a horse, or they didn't understand the speed and would panic. It took time to learn the speeds of modern life; and the opposite was also true. Returning from Afghanistan, many foreigners had a hard time readapting to a fast-paced life. There was so much noise; it was all so fast.

Back in the U.S., I once heard a train at night. I was informed that no one else heard it, as it was a mile away. So it seemed to me that you could slow down from a fast paced environment to a slower one, say go from the U.S. to Afghanistan, and some senses and abilities seemed enhanced. But it seemed harder to come from a slower paced world and adapt to a rapid, modern one.

## ❧ 34 ❧

# Foreigners as Amusement

Sometimes it felt that we *horagis*, foreigners, though overall graciously welcomed and treated well, were there for a different reason unbeknownst to us. Sometimes, especially after a series of mishaps, one began to suspect that we were imported in order to amuse the people.

We varied greatly, from the individual Westerners out to explore, to the bus-traveling Soviets or Chinese always grouped and always monitored and watched by their own security. Our actions were interesting to Afghans, often incomprehensible, and at times silly and stupid.

And often it was funny, and the story of our antics world be told and retold, city to village, village to village, again and again over cups of tea on a rug in a garden, or under quilts next to a charcoal brazier in the winter, or on a bus or in a shared taxi on a journey.

"... You know they blow their noses into handkerchiefs and then put them into their pockets—ugh!" For them this is the equivalent of saving your toilet paper.

"... And they put food into their mouths using their left hand!" This hand was reserved only for toilet functions.

"... You should see how uncomfortable the men get if you hold their hand. It's so funny, the longer you hold their hand the more nervous they get and then their faces turn so red!" Shaking hands and holding was viewed as just basic human warmth, a sign of friendship.

# ☙ 35 ❧

# Mountains

Mountains are Afghanistan. There are great plains but one is never far from mountains in your eyes or in your mind's eye. And these mountains are not of one kind—they range—climbing up to Tirich Mir at 26,000 feet, land of the famous travel book *A Short Walk in the Hindu Kush*. Some are low and soft mounds upon mounds, other are sharp cliffs, some are huge piles of rubble-like stones, others twisted veins and strata of rock that pile up upon each other—blinding, snow-capped, and glacial, barren brown and gray, or Nuristani green.

Some are straight out of a Persian miniature, jagged, sharp, rising steeply—surreal fantasies. The mountain ranges are tough, massive, and always have a wild air.

People live on them in countless villages perched on stone terraces laboriously built up on steep slopes; some are like eagles' nests. Others live on the barren slopes above the lines carved into the hillsides—the irrigation canals that water green terraced fields below. Others live at the valley edges or on the valley floor, safe in the surrounding irrigated greenery.

Since the mountains were everywhere, I assumed that their presence was everywhere in the people's culture and psyche, and that they were a source of love and inspiration. Throughout the world, be it Switzerland, Japan, the American West, or elsewhere, mountains have been heartfelt symbols of freedom, courage, home.

One day at a picnic I halfheartedly asked some people what they thought and felt about the mountains. I later asked many others. The answer I got then, and which was repeated in various ways many times, was brief, and shocking to me. Hamid said, "They make us *dek*, sad." Another explained that they preferred to be with people, with their families, that the mountains were "empty." Others said that they were so "lonely"—wild animals live there, and thieves hide up there, *jinns*, spirits, strange things happen there too; there are snakes that fly and attack you, and *modare reals*—wild people-like creatures.

The mountains made many feel alone, empty, very, very raw; they were threatening. They—the people, with their families, with others—were "civilization," the "known," against the wild, "the unknown."

Now, there were some people who had the opposite view, who cherished their peaks and were inspired by them. But the natural dangers that mountains posed in an earthquake-prone country with very few emergency services—landslides, avalanches, even just a falling rock, plus animals and thieves, real or imagined—these were very real threats. I could understand them, yet I was very surprised by their feelings towards the mountains they lived in. They did not inspire freedom and individualism. They actually seemed to bind people closer together to their family, clan, and tribal roots.

# ᎘ 36 ᎚

# From Faizabad

O nce I took one of those converted buses, built on a truck chassis, coming back from Faizabad in the province of Badakhshan, in the far northeast. It is a sleepy, dusty town in brown, rounded, very high and steep hills along the banks of the swift, glacial Kokcha River. This feeds into the Amu Darya—the Oxus—one of the fabled rivers of Central Asia, downstream. It is the border between Afghanistan, Tajikistan, and Uzbekistan. Badakhshan is a large, remote province, sparsely populated. The Hindu Kush slopes down from the south to the north. In the east is higher terrain and the panhandle, the Wakhan, that divides Tajikistan from Pakistan and touches China's Xinjiang province. This long stretch was given to Afghanistan to serve as a buffer zone between the British and Russian Empires.

Actually the whole country served this purpose, a major reason for its independence. Kyrgyz people lived in this panhandle. The Wakhan is a 17,000-foot high valley, ruled at that time by Rahman Qul, a sort of personage in the country. Wild, huge Marco Polo sheep were competing with these people for existence, and losing. A foresighted plan was set up to ensure both groups' survival. Hunters, who paid ten to fifteen thousand dollars, could then come in for a "safari." This money would pay for the expedition, and some of it went for local guides, food, and pack animals—thus feeding the local economy and ensuring local help and support in conserving the animal population.

It worked, except that Rahman Qul was not the nice fellow that everyone thought him to be. I saw him once in Kabul with his distinctive Kyrgyz hat, coming out of my Kashmiri landlord's house. His son had gone with a Japanese expedition to Wakhan, and Rahman was returning the visit. Old issues of *National Geographic* mention him as being involved in the drug trade in western China in the 1940s. Under Mao, people into drugs were shot. Rahman was a wanted man across the border, and he would have been shot on sight. But in Afghanistan, he was still a tribal chief, kind to foreigners, but harsher with his own people. During the war, Rahman's people fled over the passes to lowland Pakistan. There they languished in the heat and dust. He applied to move his people en mass to Alaska. This request was denied and some ended up not so happily in Turkey. Many stayed in Afghanistan.

At the entrance to this corridor lived the Wakhi people. Now, Afghans grew the poppies that produced opium, but they rarely used it themselves. They left it to the Persians and to the peoples of the subcontinent who used it in various ways. They preferred their chars, hashish. The story goes that somehow these Wakhi people started using opium. And as opium is a very subtle drug, they gradually found themselves addicted to it. Some sold herds, lands, possessions, and some sold even their children to finance their addiction.

Badakhshan, along with much of the north, is inhabited by Tajiks, mostly Ismaili Muslims, related to the people of Tajikistan and many city dwellers of the Central Asian nations, especially Uzbekistan. In Faizabad I was told that it was once an independent kingdom with its own symbol—an upward pointed scimitar. It was old, part of the Silk Road territory. There were Greek ruins. Ay Khanum was one such ruined city on the high banks of the Oxus, excavated by the French, bulldozed by the Taliban. In the northeast was a lake called Lake Shewa. Someone told me that it was named after the Hindu Lord Shiva when the Aryan Hindus were crossing the mountains towards India. It was also said to have Greek ruins on its shores. I never got that far to see.

Badakhshan's big claim to fame in world history is that it is the major source of lapis lazuli, the blue stone. You find it used lavishly next to gold and turquoise in ancient Egyptian art. This trade route was thousands of miles long. Ground up, lapis was said to have been used in the glaze of the best tile work. It colored miniature paintings, and European medieval and Renaissance artists used it in their vivid blues. It can be dark or lighter, solid color or with gold flecks. It is mined in a remote valley on the north slopes of the Hindu Kush. Off limits, government controlled, it was said to be a dangerous place, said to be mined by prisoners, said to be a harsh, primitive operation. Today it is still mined, still using simple technology.

Nonetheless the area has supplied the world for millennia. I bought some pieces in Kabul, was told Americans preferred it with gold flecks, Germans dark blue, each to his own. What is strange is that the wealth it produced never seemed to have led to the development of a local center of power—no city or fortresses. The site was remote, the lapis mined and carried to centers of power, or traded elsewhere.

After a visit to the area, I took one of the trucks-turned-buses from Faizabad to Kunduz. The chassis had a metal bus shell, boldly painted on the outside with flowers and framed postcard scenes. Inside were homemade, hard wooden seats. The front was sectioned off for women. The back was filled with men, boys, and bags and boxes of goods, even chickens. The roof had piles of bags and rugs. Windows were glass, not safety glass. It was a bumpy and loud ride. The dirt road was cut into the side of the cliffs a hundred feet above the rapid, green-blue glacial Kokcha River, no guardrails, no nothing. Everyone said a prayer and we started off. It was about one vehicle wide, with wider areas here and there. When we met a vehicle coming from the opposite direction, they or we would back up this curving road and then narrowly pass. I was seated on a bench on the right side near the back door. I initially felt this was good, as I could escape if . . . . But gradually, as we stopped and accepted more passengers, the doorway filled with baggage and people. If we fell into the river, it would all be fairly quick: the fall, the freezing water, the swift current, and who knew how deep the river was—well, there was not much chance of survival.

I thought of the dead buses I had seen at the bottom of the deep gorges, the Tangi Garu, leading out of Kabul—they were so small down there. And there were no ambulances, no emergency services, no phones. Only passers-by could help, and their presence depended on luck. And what they could do was next to nothing. So I sat, cozily jammed next to others, aware that escape was blocked, yet strangely feeling comfort in sharing my fate with others. We were together as we moved in narrow stretches of road; rocks would fall into the river or sometimes we would scrape against the rock wall. Once, a small bush on the cliff side flipped in and out of an open window. There was a snake on it. Though it remained entwined on the bush, people screamed and screamed.

We came to a bridge over a stream that fed into the river. It was built of logs, rocks, and dirt. Logs were wedged into the sides of both cliffs, then others laid on top, jutting out further across the chasm, weighed down by rocks; then other logs were laid down jutting out further until this cantilevered structure spanned the chasm. It was one lane wide and vehicles waited, alternating their crossings. Our turn came; some people jumped out, engine off, everyone began to pray, then silence. The driver positioned us at the bridge and then backed up. He revved the engine, again and again.

He sped across and stopped. Rocks fell from the bridge down into the gorge. The prayers of thanksgiving were loud. We walked across and reboarded.

At one stop, a group of soldiers asked for a ride. After some discussion they climbed on the roof with their baggage. And the rounded roof of the bus now bent down concave. It was ominous. We kept going. One area we passed through looked like endless sand dunes, except that they were huge round brown hills with endless earth, no rock, with the road twisting over and around them. It was massive and surreal, mound next to mound, stretching in all directions as far as we could see—high brown steep hills endless, repeating.

Much later we stopped at a teahouse for the night, ate oily rice, drank tea, and slept on the raised platforms they call sofas. Being more than tired by the day's journey, I foolishly washed my face in the cold water of an irrigation canal across the road. It looked so cool and clear and felt wonderful, refreshing. I dunked my head in it and felt alive again; the brown dust and numbness went away. Just a little water on me brought me back to life and a vivid appreciation of the life around me—the wonder of green grass by the canal—the flowers, the birds—the excitement of just sitting and drinking a cup of tea! From that delicious water, I later came down with giardia, which makes you burp and pass gas the smell of rotten eggs and amoeba, and also makes you very weak. The medication makes you feel even worse.

Once we reached the plains closer to Kunduz, we hit a dust storm. The sky and air were amber brown colored and everything got covered with it, the insides of nose and mouth filled with the grit, despite cloths across our faces. It was beautiful like a blizzard, only all was a tawny brown and it was quieting to realize that these storms covered large areas, and destroyed the ecosystem. As in great storms or earthquakes, one is humbled in helplessness in the face of nature.

# ☙ 37 ☙

# Yogurt

Yogurt, or *mast*, is a staple of the diet and delicious in all its forms. The king and queen had an experimental farm outside Kabul, complete with modern barn and silos that were open to the public. Here, the milk was pasteurized and safe and for sale.

Most milk in the country was suspect; cows could be tubercular or carry brucellosis or other diseases. Yogurt, because of boiling and fermentation, is considered safe. Every home makes its own; tastes therefore vary considerably. I especially remember the yogurt I was served by the Kuchi nomads, strong and tart. Mixed with cucumbers and mint, it cooled you in the hot summers. Mixed with walnuts and raisins, it was supposed to warm you in winter. And because it was full of various bacterial cultures, it was very helpful to the health of the otherwise suffering people.

It was served with almost all meals and was especially good with *aushak*, leek-filled ravioli-like dumplings. It was also used to cool hot, spicy dishes.

Rug merchants would cover rugs with it and then leave them in the sun to dry. This process would cause the colors to fade to a more "antique" look. When it was dry, it could be brushed out.

It is also dried into small, rock-hard lumps called *kroot*, a great, easy way to store it until it was reconstituted with liquid for cooking.

Yogurt, with its bacterial cultures, no doubt, helps keep the country alive since most people had one or more severe intestinal problems. Periodically or when we were ill, we would hand in stool samples. The doctor always knew when someone would hand in a

servant's or Afghan friend's stool in order to get treatment. Instead of the one or two ailments the Westerner might have, the Afghan would likely have three, four, or more.

Because of these debilitating problems, a full day's labor is difficult to perform. Yes, people worked hard, but a full day's labor is very tiring. And people aged quickly. But then, 50 percent of the children died before the age of twelve. So, if you survived this, you generally had a good chance of living much longer.

## ᥱ 38 ᥱ

# The Rommel

Mahmoud wanted to have his fortune told. So four of us went to see a fortune teller in the old city who used a very special method to divine the future. There were many people and many ways to do this. There were birds or monkeys who picked out cards with your future on them. Some people read cards. Others read your palm. There were what we would call psychics. Various dream interpretations were used. But Mahmoud wanted to go to a man who used a method he had only heard of. Enthusiastically he gathered several of us together and off we went towards the old city.

Near the river we entered the maze of car-less adobe-walled alleys and then asked our way. Down a narrow alley we came to an open door, with windows to our right. Inside was a small, low, dim room at alley level. A thin elderly man with old, round glasses stood and greeted us and invited us in.

Unusually, he was seated not on the floor but at a wooden table with several old chairs lined up facing the door. He told us to sit on the rickety chairs. The entire room was adobe colored, and the door and furniture were weathered brown. His clothes, his hat, everything, were these colors except for a few small colored prints on the wall. On the table were several old, worn books. We introduced ourselves and explained what we all wanted. He agreed to help us. Now he used an ancient device as a means of divination.

The *Rommel* have two pieces. Each consisted of four brass-colored metal dice, said to be made of a multitude of special elements, some say 200. A rod ran through them and kept them together as they rotated on it. Each of the four sides of each die had a number of dots incised into the surface, one, two, three, four.

He explained the procedure and in turn each of us went up to him and did what we were told. He consulted his books and then gave the reading. To each he said the usual positive things—you will marry, have many sons, etc., and then added a caution—advice that if not followed, would bring ill fortune. He was pleasant and explained in a kind way but when he got to the last part, his demeanor changed and he seemed a different person. He spoke with authority and strength—and looked directly in the person's eye.

When my turn came, he placed the Rommel between my hands. He told me to rub them, thus rotating the cubes. Then I threw them on the mat on the table. He counted up the dots on the top sides of the eight dice and noted which die had which number of dots. Then he consulted his books and calculated and pondered. And then, somewhat alarmed, he very emphatically began to insist that I get married as soon as possible. We discussed, but he was adamant. In fact he said he knew a marriage broker (yes, there are such things), and could arrange it for that afternoon. I said I didn't know the person. He said no matter, he would easily find a woman. He then added that if I didn't get married immediately I most certainly never would. His face was severe—not to marry was like death—no wife! No children! In Islam one must marry.

Who would take care of me? My friends had less dramatic fortunes.

## ❦ 39 ❧

# They

The majority of Afghans are Sunni of different schools. Others are Shia—Hazaras, people in the west of the country, and many Kabulis. Others were Ismailis, others belonged to various other religious groups. There were Hindus and Sikhs and a few members of other denominations. Many Muslims also follow various teachers or join one of the many Sufi orders. So one might be Sunni yet follow very esoteric teachings from a Sufi or other leader. Despite this complex pattern of allegiances and beliefs, minority groups faced problems and at times persecution and massacres. Certain groups, because of past persecutions, developed theological devices that allowed them to deny their beliefs in public, if necessary, for their survival.

There is the Arabic term, *tarqiyya*. Under this term one can basically lie to protect their religion, the *ummah*, their community. Traditionally it was used when one was under persecution, danger of death—a logical idea. But moderate Muslim friends say with great dismay and frustration that it is now being used by a few immigrants in the West to say things like, yes, they believe in the Western government and support it, even though privately they do not and instead work to promote their own agenda of Sharia law or to qualify for increased social benefits, or to say a second wife is a sister, and so on.

One of the less favored groups were the Ismailis, followers of the Agha Khan. Early breakaways from the Shia, they are now found worldwide and are noted for their hospitals and education projects. In Afghanistan they traditionally lived in the high mountains, mostly in northeast Badakhshan, or in some cities. Clearly in the past they found refuge in these isolated areas from very real dangers.

There is a story that at one time in the Middle East, during massive persecutions of their faith, their fortress, center, and precious libraries were all plundered and destroyed by the Mongols. It was in Afghanistan, in remote Badakhshan, that some of their most prized volumes survived.

Mahmoud was full of stories, and one day over tea he said, "You outsiders"—foreigners—"don't know what these other groups do".

You think it is just another group of our religion. It's not so— they are *kafir*, unbelievers." When I countered with what I had read, he shook his head as if to dust off my words. His eyes narrowed, and he said that there had been a family that was appointed to rule over and look after the people as local representatives of the Agha Khan, their supreme leader. They lived at that time on the north side of the Hindu Kush mountains. Supposedly some years ago this leader invited the king, Zahir Shah, to a *shekar*, a hunt. In this part of the world this means that people spread out over a large area and slowly, beating drums, making noise, shouting, drive the game towards a central area where the hunters are waiting to shoot the panicked animals. These people are called beaters. Because of the political situation at the time, this leader wanted to impress the king, to show that his people were good subjects, orderly, helpful when needed, that they were civil and were absolutely no threat to his majesty. He called for his people to come to help with the hunt, to act as beaters. One hundred thousand people assembled! The shekar was a huge success, scores of animals were shot, and the king was lavishly entertained. His majesty was duly impressed, thanked his host, and returned to the capital. In Kabul the officials—Sunni and Shia—were, like most, deeply prejudiced against these people and against this family. Where the people had wanted to show their loyalty, these Kabulis saw only what they wanted to see—a potential source of opposition, a powerful lord who could command large numbers of people.

Now, there were other tribal and religious leaders who had more power, but these people were different, they felt—not to be trusted. So the next time the leader came to Kabul, he was entertained by the king graciously. At the end, when he was about to return to his home in the north, he was "invited" by his majesty to "remain in Kabul" so that his majesty could more easily enjoy his company—and so he stayed. An eye could be kept on him more easily here, and he and his family could be more easily controlled.

"And then, as if this was not enough," Mahmoud said, "they do terrible things".

"Like what?" I said.

Well, it was too terrible, he answered. After prodding, he said that he had been told this, and that everyone knew but no one could stop them because these leaders are so secretive. He said, "You know the way we pray, men together in rows, this was developed in early Islam during jihad, like soldiers, facing Mecca, usually privately but on Fridays all together in the mosques—and the women usually privately but sometimes in a separate section in the mosque."

"Yes," I said, "I have seen, I know."

"Well," he said, "they don't do this."

"How do you know?"

"Everybody knows," he said. And his cousin knew some of these tribal and religious leaders and said it was true.

According to him, the people meet privately to pray in large rooms. No outsiders are allowed. And here his eyes narrowed, and then said with grave sternness and disgust—"they pray men and women together!"

When I answered with "So, we Christians and Jews and Hindus and all do too," he answered with his eyes—a look of pity and revulsion that we did such an impure, such a dirty act and thought nothing of it. He then firmly stated that it was unclean. It was haram, forbidden, but there was more. He said that they met at night and did this polluted prayer, "And then," he said, eyes wide, "they put out the oil lamps, the candles, the electric light—whatever, and then in the darkness they all have sex with each other. They don't know who they are touching because it is dark. Mom with sister, father with daughter, anyone! No one knows anyone. And then someone tells them to stop, they do, and then go home. Horrible," he said.

I said I didn't believe such a story. He countered with "You foreigners . . . ." He said, "They do these things. It is true." He added that when there was a wedding that the bride had to spend her first night with the leader of the community if he so desired, not with her husband, that this was the law with "them." I countered that I had heard of this custom before but it had been in reference to great khans, lords, all over the country, and I mentioned Mahmoud's tribal roots. It was also done years ago in many countries. To this he blushed and said yes, he had heard the same but that it could not be true.

It is amazing how often the orgy story had been used against minority groups. Perhaps all this viewing of things in terms of sex is just a totally understandable response in a conservative, sex-segregated society full of frustration. From that point of view, is it not logical to assume that mixed company would, of course, lead to an orgy, or that foreigners, with so little clothing on, would be promiscuous? Mahmoud understood my line of reasoning but still did not thrust "them." When I added that much of Cairo was built by them and that al-Azhar, now Sunni, the oldest Islamic university, was established by them, he stared. Then I added, "And the hospitals in Pakistan."

"I don't know," he said. "Maybe, but I still don't like them."

Interestingly nowadays the Agha Khan's charities have built schools, clinics, and hotels, and they have been massively involved with the restoration of valuable historical buildings of the country, and its cultural heritage. These sites range from Babur's Garden—the tomb of the first Mughal Emperor of India—to lesser-known shrines and tombs. Their work is unavoidable in looking at the country, and perhaps their presence will earn them some increased tolerance and respect. They have been criticized for promoting their beliefs and looking after their own interests. But what group in the country does not?

In recent times I have heard comments from Afghans and they repeated the prejudices of old and worse.

## ❧ 40 ❧

# Family Tomb

One day when I was visiting Nur Agha on his farm, he led me to the other side of the groups of compounds and walled gardens. We walked to what seemed to be a long, narrow, high-walled compound topped with tall bushy trees. As we neared the gate, we saw a man sitting on the ground to the right. He could have passed for one of the typical beggars that stationed themselves near places of prayer, mosques, tombs, but there was some very different air about him. He stood to greet Nur Agha and kissed his hand, as many did. Nur Agha didn't deal with him in the quick and direct manner he often did with the people that were always around him.

He spoke with him slowly and respectfully, clasping both his hands. I was struck by a mutuality present and a sharp feeling that yes, there were two people greeting each other but that there also was another something there. There were two men present, but there also was something else now present. It was not visible but it was clearly felt, it was there. I stared at them.

We pulled open one side of the great old wooden gate and stepped into cool garden shade. Nur Agha then turned to me and looked carefully at me. Then, perhaps judging that I had sensed something at their meeting, began to explain. He said that the man outside had been a university professor but was now a Sufi, a dervish, who lived here. He stressed that he was a real Sufi, not like all those others who pose to be. He looked into my eyes sharply when he explained this—so that I would mark the gravity of what he said. He said there were very few people like him in the country.

The long pathway was lined with rows of very tall, straight trees. "Cotton trees," he explained. "They produce a cotton-like material useful to stuff cushions, but it burns easily." The lines of tall, old trees fashioned the narrow garden into a pillared hall deeply shaded. The ground was covered with dark vegetation. At the end to the left was an old building in some disrepair—we entered and went down steps to a large, very high-ceilinged room. What was odd was the wood and matted frame that hung down from the ceiling in the middle, ropes connected to the sides. I had not seen anything like it. He explained that it was basically a huge suspended fan, the bottom of which could be pulled back and forth to create a breeze. It was what in India they call a *punkah*. The deep basement-like room could indeed be comfortable during the hot summers.

Outside again, we moved to the bright whitewashed building to the right at the end of the garden. There was a tomb and graveyard. These were family members, Nur Agha said. Traditionally, long blocks of stone or brick constructs, sculpture-like, were built on the ground, sometimes low to mark a grave. The longer the construct, the greater the saintliness of the deceased. Outside he pointed out the tombs of relatives and of his brother's children—I had not known of their losses. Then there was a low-shaped building with an Islamic style cement grill window. Inside was the long, long tomb of his grandfather, and another one of his father. I asked Nur Agha if they burned incense here—though I saw no signs of it, no holder or ashes. It was a sweet, very gentle, and soothing smell. I could not name the scent. He matter-of-factly said, "No, no incense was burned here. It is the saintliness that caused the perfume." I was skeptical, but he just repeated what he had said. Later, Italian Catholic friends said that this was common at tombs of saints.

## ༀ 41 ༁

# Women, from Queen to Kuchi

There is a world you see and there is a world that you do not see. The world of the Afghan woman is this way. There was a story that in the late sixties the king approached his wife for her permission to take a second wife. Now under Sharia, Islamic law, there are many points of law in favor of the wife. Considering the prevailing social conditions of the Arab people living in the southern part of the Arabian Peninsula at the time of the Prophet Mohammed these points were way ahead of their times.

A woman has rights to the money she brings to the marriage if she divorces later (though it is true that a man can initiate a divorce much more easily than a woman). She is entitled to support, she can give or withhold her consent for the husband marrying another wife, and she has other rights. There are, however, many other points of the law which are not favorable to women.

Of course, as in all countries, what is written as law and what is practiced is much different. A divorced woman, often scorned and threatened by her own family, has little power before the traditional male establishment. For example, there was a young man, Abdul, who was desperately trying to support his mother and young sister after his father took another wife. The wife had not wanted to give permission for the second marriage, but after some beatings she gave in and was promised support, but none was given; she could do nothing. She didn't have family backing or strong male support.

If a man had power and money, there was little recourse. If this woman had had money and male family backing, she could have taken the situation to court. However, the courts rarely rule in favor of a lone woman. In wealthy countries, but especially in poor countries, money connections allowed the unallowable.

If a wife had difficulties with her spouse, she had little recourse. If she went back to her parents, this brought shame to the family and often the father would not be welcoming. What would people say of him? I knew of a prominent educated family wherein a daughter divorced her husband because of repeated infidelities. Her father beat her screaming that she was a Pashtun wife and had to return to her husband no matter what! In a bold step for women's advancement she refused. A woman could be killed for bringing shame to the family. This was true even in wealthy, educated circles. Often men would mock other men if their wives deviated from conservative norms. And the law seemed to always bow to male pride.

In the countryside all was worse. The position of women varied from ethnic group to ethnic group, but it was always inferior to that of men. In tribal Pashtun areas you rarely saw a woman; you did not ask a man about the women in his family. They were invisible, necessary for children, namely sons, but almost a source of embarrassment. It was a man's world on the outside.

But on the inside, as in many cultures, life varied. A woman could wield great power within the home. But since marriages were usually arranged, it was not the love of a wife and husband that predominated; it was what was of benefit to the family fortunes.

I once asked a friend who was more important, a wife or a mother. In a flash, he stated "My mother!" A wife is good, but you can always get another. But you had only one mother. I was surprised by this intensity and asked others, always with the same answer. Then later I realized that it was a pattern common to many traditional countries. Of course in other countries a different world view prevails. The mother would say to the son,"I gave you birth so that you could have a life, I would die to give you life! Save your wife and raise your family".

When a typical Afghan woman marries, she usually moves to the husband's family home or compound. She enters her husband's world alone, has few allies, but eventually has her children, who become her support and assets. She especially dotes on or spoils her sons, since her ties with her husband are tenuous, and since they, her sons, will have power in the future. They will care for her. She will protect the children from the father, who has to play a patriarchal role; she will help choose her sons' wives. How many other cultures and families have this mama's boy pattern? The man's strongest loyalties are to his mother and a mother to her sons. So a wife had to curry the favor of her husband's mother, another side to the eternal mother-in-law problem.

So, the twentieth-century king asked the queen for her consent to a second wife. She, a member of the royal clan, also of the Mohammadzai Clan, was enraged. She supposedly drew the pistol she always carried and aimed at his crotch; she missed. He grabbed the gun and then grabbed a *buzkashi* whip, a short leather handle with multiple thongs used to beat your horse, or the opposing team, or your own team member during the game of buzkashi. He beat her and mangled her hand. It was then arranged that she go to Bethesda Naval Hospital in the United States for surgery to correct this. Thus he did not take a second wife. It is a story.

Senior women in a family or clan could have immense respect and power. Among rural or nomadic people there was sometimes much more freedom and mutual respect between a man and a woman. Her work was needed and valued. While working or moving, there was much more contact. When you saw women among the Kuchi, a name for Pashto-speaking nomads, you knew things were different.

Once I was involved in a TB study, to find the rate of infection in the old city. We inoculated people one week, and they would return in a week when we would read the reactions to the shot. A red mark indicated exposure to the disease. Women inoculated women; men, men.

One day the room was jammed with men and women. We gave them little gifts provided by the U.N. if they returned for the reading. We were told to give them what we had from CARE: a tube of toothpaste, a box of pudding (instructions in English). We wondered. One kindly old gentleman, a Baba, with almost no teeth pleaded for more tubes of toothpaste. We joked with him, "What do you need it for, Baba?" "Oh," he said, "it is just wonderful for my feet. They are so bad, but when I put it on, it is so good!"

Suddenly there was a commotion at the door and the crowd now parted like Moses at the Sea of Reeds. With space to the right and left, in walked a Kuchi woman, a nomad. True to her people, she wore multiple purplish-red flowered dresses, a vest, silver jewelry—no veil, no scarf. Her bold face was framed by many long, small braids of black hair that fell over her shoulders. She was regal, as all their women were, walked to the head of the women's line, and demanded an injection. She got one and then complained, "It was not good, it didn't hurt, give me another one." After some discussion, the woman vaccinator gave her another one. She left and though we explained what it was and she clearly understood, she never returned. "Not hurting" was a common complaint. We tried to be gentle, not to hurt, but this was taken as being ineffective, weak. It had to hurt if it was good.

Another time I was standing at a bus stop. A cheap truck, turned into a bus with a painted metal shell, wood benches, and glass windows, was passing and had splattered muddy water on a Kuchi woman's dress. The woman, obviously not used to city ways, had stood next to the water, where others did not. At first shocked by the suddenness of the act, she then began to curse. The bus was still moving away very slowly—it was very full—when she bent down, picked up a good-sized rock and hurled it through the window of the bus. Glass shattered; people screamed and yelled, the bus sped away. She stood tall, had her hands on her hips laughing and laughing. The men and women nearby gave her wide berth, their eyes reflected fear, admiration, and wonder. The bus did not stop and no one yelled or argued or even spoke to her—she was a Kuchi woman.

City people said that every Kuchi woman carried a dagger and was not shy in using it; contrast these ladies with city women in chador that rarely left their homes! It actually was the same with horagi, foreign women living there. Some were fearful of venturing even to the older parts of Kabul, which were safe. Then there were the women Peace Corps vaccinators who traveled on horseback for weeks to vaccinate women and children in remote mountainous areas, areas that had no roads, only trails, and had never seen a horagi, an outsider. They said they had "a great time," and relished getting out of the city and back to work in the hinterland.

## ❧ 42 ☙

# How They Built the Big Dome

Several people told me similar versions of a story about how the large blue-tiled dome on the Pul-e Khishti Mosque in central Kabul was built. There was an old mosque on the site, but in the 1960s it was rebuilt. It didn't have the open courtyard plan commonly found in this area of the world. The weather here is harsher, so the courtyard area was covered by a large blue-tiled dome. The building was on the banks of the Kabul River by the Pul-e Khishti, or "brick bridge," in the central old part of Kabul. There was open area around it and then arcaded shops whose rent was used for the mosque's upkeep, a practical plan common in the Islamic world. It was a block-like building covered with white-gray marble with the big blue dome and one tall minaret capped with a little blue cupola. It blended a Turkish domed mosque with blue tile in the Central Asian way.

It was the biggest dome in the country and after it was constructed, various people, not present when it was built, tried to understand how it had been done. One man, an otherwise educated middle-class person, was not present then either, but I heard him tell his family this story.

The builders had a problem trying to find a way to span the space. Wood supports were considered but found to be too costly.

The old tradition of the master builders who created the great structures of the past had been broken, from the master builders who created the great structures of the past. No one knew "how to," anymore. The debates went on and on. Finally an old man came forth and said he could construct the dome in so many days but his instructions must be followed explicitly. And he would do this for a certain exorbitant price. It was all or nothing. If the dome was not completed by a certain date then he would not be paid. After a lot of debate his terms were accepted. He then ordered earth to be brought in and piled up higher and higher until it reached the desired level of the dome.

The earth was then formed into the shape of the dome and the bricks and masonry were laid over this and formed into the desired shape. Everyone was pleased except there was one big problem. The time limit was about up, only one day to go. If the deal was to be completed and the price paid, the huge amount of earth would have to be removed basically overnight. The old man said it would be done. At the end of the workday, the workers were sent home puzzled.

The leaders of the mosque were smiling. They had their dome, and clearly all that earth could not be moved overnight, thus the contract would be void—and they would not have to pay his high price. They also figured that then some of the money could be used to haul the earth out, and there still would be a lot of money left over. But others believed differently. Everyone went to bed with their own vision of what they would find tomorrow. The next morning early, people got up and made their way to the mosque. There they found people milling about very excitedly. People said that the earth inside the building has disappeared! How was it possible? What had happened?

The dome was still here but all the earth had been removed. The floor was clean, and the old man could not be found. Where was he? Who was he? He must have had jinns do the work for him. ("Jinni" is their term for our word "genie"). Yes, yes, jinns! Every time I heard this story or other odd tales the group of people I was with and who heard the story would nod their heads, yes, yes, and invoked Bismillahs (Blessed be the name of God) and other religious sayings. I was always amazed. Some of the groups were college educated, engineers, and business people. Later I asked one of the groups if they believed the teller's story. "Oh no, but he's older. No, but maybe, but he's older, maybe he knows more than we do, yes . . . . and we must respect him." "But why doesn't anyone tell the truth?" I asked.

"It would be disrespectful to him," one person said. "Allah can do this . . . .".

Another version says that when the dome was finished the old master builder told the poor neighborhoods of the city that silver and gold coins had been hidden in the earth under the dome. People rushed to dig out pails full of earth to search for the coins. Coins were found and the earth was removed.

Keeping up respect and preserving honor takes many forms. I've heard many stories from Afghans in the diaspora who tell of "peaceful homes," where the parents are respected and deferred to and treated well. But when the children went out, they got into all sorts of trouble, and when the parents found out, they were shocked, but again no one talked about it. The children sometimes were taught to treat their parents formally—so they never confided in them or even shared their problems with them. Everything looks good but then problems with school or the police would arise and the parents were surprise. Then after the initial drama, the dynamics would go back to the way they were before: "all looks well." Parents must be respected.

The traditional roles are played out on the surface but there is sometimes little real communication in the space between these roles. Great effort is expended to maintain "the form", to make things look good. But as an Afghan teacher proclaimed,"how can problems be fixed if you cannot talk about them?"

## ❧ 43 ❧

# The Split Father

Late one afternoon I asked Nur Agha about his late father. Even though he was young he was a very respected spiritual leader because he took his beliefs seriously. (His uncle, being senior was head of the family now.) Nur's Father, older and head of the whole family, and spiritually inclined had been held in much higher respected. People said that he had had a drinking problem and had four wives, the legal Muslim maximum, but also had the legal number of the different levels of sub-wives and was known for his very worldly ways.

I could see how his hereditary title was just a happenstance of birth. He was born into a family with position, like a royal, fit for it or not. In his case they were religious titles. Many viewed him as a living saint or as a person with powers since he was a descendant of one of the greatest saints in Islam, and as the oldest male he held the mantle, or authority. But Nur Agha had told me that his father was a deeply spiritual man. This did not fit with the stories that were told about him, which seemed to be true, given the large number of Nur Agha's siblings. So I asked which or what was the truth.

When I asked my question, I really was not sure how he would respond. I did feel somewhat safe doing so; it was part of my role, who I was, being an "outsider," a horagi. I could say things and ask things that most Afghans could not. Also it's a bit of my personality, to probe, to try to understand. I would not be subject to

176

Afghan social punishment, but I could lose a very dear friend. Yet the question was haunting me and Nur always encouraged honesty. The worst that could happen was that I would not be invited to return; our friendship would be ended.

When I posed my question, Nur suddenly looked colder, serious, there was a silence. I was not sure what would happen next. I was looking at him but felt that I was actually looking not at him but through him. Looking through a window. He was not there.

Then suddenly, "*Doroost!* True!" he said. His father had had these problems but he also said that what he had told me of him was also true. "*Ee tur ast*, it is like this. Daytime was hard for him. So hard to deal with everydayness, to deal with the realities of all the problems people came to him to solve for them—family problems, money, work, political, spiritual problems. Crowds of people came to him everyday. Every morning the outer courtyard would be full of such people. Later in the day more important people would come for appointments, so many, even the King would come. The King would come to him, he did not go to the King. The day was a time of constant difficulties, constant requests for help of some kind, constant work. So he needed ways to escape from this chaos during the day. He needed the opposite experiences, escape, so he smoked, he drank, and had wives, and yes! —it was hard for him to balance "This with 'That.'"

At this Nur's face suddenly beamed, smiling, his eyes huge. "But at night! At night! *Khoda!* Khoda, Khoda, God, God, God . . . " These words were part of the Sufi exercises he was doing at night with his followers—*zikr*, spiritual exercises, with his dervishes and Sufis and others. Various Sufi groups do various practices in order to try to touch, experience God. Some whirl, do art, dance, his did powerful breathing exercises. These were intense, passionate; one abandoned one's self.

So the story was not so simple. Ecstatic experiences at night, the closeness of spiritual partnership, were very strong and consuming. These nights being so extraordinary, how could one deal with the mundane?

Evidently in order to deal with the daytime, he needed to numb up, to have less feelings, to be less aware. It was not just that perhaps he was psychologically a person who needed a lot of stimulation, sensation. No, this is too limiting a view of the range and depth of life.

No, when we have experiences, and we all do, that touch the vastness of life, that touch the great Love, then it is so hard to deal with the rest, the here and now, the today. We rarely speak of them.

True, these experiences stretch us, expose us, but so little of our usual normal world teaches us how to deal with this or even makes space for us socially and personally to have such experiences. Who talks about them? Certainly not most people, not the TV or papers, and too often not the religious either. They are too busy organizing, or doing good deeds.

Yet these experiences are not something rare, freaky, or monastic: they are common to all and open to all. But people have them and usually do not know what to do with them, don't know how to integrate them into their own lives. Perhaps the high rate of alcoholism and drug addiction, overeating, addiction to the Internet and other technology toys, and other compulsions are evidence of people's attempts to numb themselves to experiences they do not know what to do with. They are left alone with no one to talk to.

# Some Notes From Herat

In the west of the country on the road to the immensely rich holy Shia shrine city of Mashad, Iran, is the antient city of Herat. The world often jokes of the wealth of the Vatican, most of it frozen in art, while ignoring the colossal highly secret worth of the Islamic shrines in Mecca, Najaf, Mashad, Qom, and other places, and of the similar staggering wealth of the major Hindu temples and Buddhist temples. For centuries pilgrims have donated gold, jewels, land, and valuables to these shrines. In Iran people say that when the government in Tehran wants to make a major decision it must first consult with the shrine in Mashad. The domes of the shrine are gold plated, not gold leafed.

Herat was one of Alexander the Great's "Alexandrias." It is situated in a broad valley on the banks of the Hari Rud, the Hari River. Though originally settled centuries earlier, the predominant old structures surviving in the city are buildings of the Timurid period (1369–1509). The old city was laid out as a square with two major roads intersecting in the center, roughly dividing it into four quarters, like a Roman military camp or an ideal Hindu city. Of course the city spread out beyond its old walls. Not much is left of them after modernization, but old photos show beautifully sculptured massive slanted walls that tapered up, like something out of a fairy tale or a science fiction movie. These people are proud of their culture and of education.

North of the city on the slopes of hills were ruins, shrines, gardens, whose sites were selected because of the views. Leaving the old city on the way to this area, you passed the tomb of Gawhar Shad, a Timurid queen, the builder of the Mashad Shrines, with a fluted, ribbed blue tile dome, the vaulted interior intricately painted in arabesques, which along with the minarets are the sole remnants of a large religious complex. Now the tiles have fallen off the dome and minarets; now they are bare and brown, innocent victims of the fighting. The fighting and the busy highway next to them have shaken them loose.

I once climbed a rickety metal ladder to enter a hole in the side of a minaret in hopes of findings stairs to climb higher. Once in I found it too awkward to contort myself up to where the stairs began. But when I started to climb out I found I had to lay face down and push my legs far out before I could then bend for my feet to find the ladder. I froze and suddenly realized that here in Central Asia there were no available tall ladders or professional help to call. It as stark. Of course reality gradually entered my brain and I faced my vertigo and got back to earth.

To the north of the city up on a dry, barren slope was a small brick shrine, typically Timurid in style: a large, pointed, open vault , like an English Tutor arch, with smaller side vaults, facing a walled courtyard. In this, to the left as you entered was a terrace with a tomb made of marble fragments, and then down some steps was the remainder of the enclosure—a level gravel yard. Parallel and near the tomb is a slight depression, as if for a body, with a chunk of white marble for a pillow. A caretaker and his family lived simply in part of the building.

This is the tomb of Khwaja Galton, a holy man who came to the city of the poets—Ansari, Jami and others—and supposedly said of himself that he "was unworthy to walk in such a place," so he rolled on the ground. And some say he died on this spot. There is an old tradition of ascetics rolling from place to place, still done in India.

The ritual in this place is you lie down in this slight depression, your head on the chunk of marble, hands over your face. The caretaker is standing there and gives you a slight nudge. Some people roll over the gravel to the right, some straight ahead, some to the left, some simply do not roll. I heard many stories that foreign engineer types, skeptical, measured to see if there was a concealed slope—none was ever found.

I saw people roll—slow, fast, right, left, and center, partially or all the way to the walls—or not roll at all. The caretaker would try to be there to buffer you from hitting the wall too hard. It was always interesting to see skeptical friends lie down, often with a great deal of protests and then roll, stop, uncover their eyes with amazed looks on their faces. An Afghan friend didn't roll at all but then it was, he said, because he was from a religious family with more power than the Khwaja, maybe.

Now people had various interpretations for what "your roll" meant. Some claimed that you had to have a wish when you lay down and if one rolled straight, then the wish would come true.

When Ali fell in love with Maryam he went to roll—he rolled straight! His wish would come true. Rolling to either side, it would not. Others said that it was a measure of one's spiritual development. How open were you to the unknown—to God? The more open, the faster. To this direction, good—to that, a warning. Others said it all reflected the power of the saint.

Of all the times I rolled, I recall my first roll best. I was curious and since I hadn't seen anyone else do it, I didn't know what to expect. I lay down in the depression; the man placed my hands over my face, said a prayer, and gave me a slight nudge at my shoulder. I moved and then felt that I was falling through space and could hear only what sounded like a loud wind, a rush, then my shoulder hit the wall. The man had run to try stopping me. Friends said they had yelled for me to slow because of the wall, but I did not hear them. I had heard only that rush. It was the same every time.

Reasons? There are "mystery spots" in many places in the world, where perspective and gravity seem distorted. It could be, except here there was only rolling and one's own experience.

Further east along this ridge overlooking the city were ruins of Timurid gardens and pavilions. In the past many wrote, enraptured of these enchanted pleasure gardens. Their beauty inspired poets and lovers. Babur Shah, founder of the Mughal Dynasty of India, the dynasty that eventually produced the Taj Mahal, spoke in his *Baburnama* (autobiography) of being drunk in one of the pavilions. The Bagh-e Umomi, Garden of the People, was partly restored. Large terraces, wooded on either side, framed a view of Herat past step-like levels of geometric flower beds and lawns, going down, down.

Water channels cascaded down beside walkways, irrigating the plots in each terrace. In the old days ceramic tile would have decorated the pavilions, with carpets, cushions laid out and curtains hung to ensure privacy. Tents were often set up in gardens—the legacy of nomadic days. They ensured shelter and privacy yet were open to the garden and allowed you to be "in" the garden instead of observing it. Sitting on carpets next to blooming flowers rising from sunken plots is totally different from looking at them while standing or from a distance or from a bench. You are close to the flowers. You smell them, see their individuality, see them moving, each differently to the wind. Having tent pavilions in gardens is like having the vigor and freshness of camping mixed with the beauties and delights of civilization, of cultivated flowers, water, and trees.

Yet further east was the shrine built to honor the poet saint Ansari. It is called Gazar Gah. Actually the site seems to have been a shrine, or religious place for millenniums, prehistoric. There was a small village, home of the *mirs* of Gazar Gah, the descendants. Timur had moved artists around to stimulate new forms. Timurid remnants included an octagonal tower, called the pepper shaker, a domed building with exquisite interior paintings of gold and lapis blue said to have been done by an itinerant Italian artisan, and a large courtyarded building, with remnants of beautiful tile work. And in the courtyard, old tombstones, a red bud tree, and a very tall iwan, a threesided vaulted hall, with peach-colored decoration said to be a Chinese touch, in which was a large cage-like structure covering the saint's tomb, and a very old tree. As everywhere there, nails or pieces of cloth were affixed to the tree or structure representing requests, pleas for the saint's intercession. In a side room was a black very intricately carved rectangular tombstone. One of the gravestones in the courtyard had a beautiful Arabic inscription, a Bismillah—"Blessed be the name of God, the Almighty, the Compassionate"—an Islamic saying constantly invoked. These words were carved along the inside of a circle, divided by the calligraphy into four equal arms, which formed a design that to a westerner looked like a Greek Eastern Christian cross, consciously done or a matter of basic design? This Bismillah was a mandala in the shape of a Greek cross. In the Eastern Christian churches the cross is not used as in the West, a focus on suffering and death, but to move one to the rest of the story—resurrection. So the cross is decorated, stylized, a celebration that it is empty—similar to this stone. In the past there were Christian communities in these areas. This was the territory of the Nestorian church, which stretched all the way into China, about which little is written. Other reports told of Christian/Muslim villages in the area. There were many unusual things in the area. The eight-hundred-year-old, two-hundred-foot Minaret of Jam, standing alone in a narrow canyon, upriver from Herat, is covered with beautiful brick calligraphy of the Sura from the Qur'an about Mary only; no one knows why. Only a few ruins and a Jewish cemetery lie nearby. Once in Herat I bought a "tasbeh", prayer beads. But they were not beads, it was a flat stone fish cut into sections instead of beads. The fish is not an Islamic symbol but it has been used as a Christian one. One one could explain it's meaning to me. One should also remember that the city is far from the Indian Ocean and has only a smallish river. There is so much fascinating history for Afghans to explore.

The architect of Gazar Gah was much praised for his work and was told that he could be buried in the sacred confines of the courtyard. It is said that he asked instead that a stone he carved into the shape of a kneeling dog be placed outside, facing the doorway even below the steps leading to the entrance, as he was too unworthy to be so near such a saint. In Islam a dog is traditionally viewed as a lowly, dirty animal, often mistreated, except for hunting dogs and except by the nomadic peoples. So, all who enter pass by "this dog." He was just a "dog"—thIS itself is a poem.

There were many ruins in and around the city. Gawhar Shad's ruined Musalla complex, mentioned above, was once said to rival the Taj Mahal, even in its ruined state. There was once an offer to have it restored.

In the 1970's the Shahbanu, Empress, of Iran was very involved in reviving the old culture and handcraft of her country. In this part of the world, rulers usually did not maintain the buildings of previous rulers, each new ruler preferring to focus on his or her own new structures. The short-lived Pahlavi dynasty of Iran (Reza Shah and his son) was actually very good about restoration, and they had two angels working for them, Dr. Arthur Upham Pope and his wife. They undertook a vast documentation of Persian art and architecture. His *Survey of Persian Art*, of many volumes, is a classic. Over the centuries, with little maintenance, much of the tile work on old buildings had fallen off. Pictures of even the buildings on the great Square in Isfahan show white washed walls. Reza Shah employed the Popes to support the training of craftsmen to massively retile these great structures. Mostly mosques that later became the meeting places for opposition to the dynasty and its eventual overthrow—ironic. The Popes had requested to be buried in Esfahan because of their love for Persian culture. The Shah allowed this and had a small beautiful brick tomb built for them in thanks for their great work. During the Islamic Revolution, their tomb was broken into and their bones were literally thrown to the dogs because they were *kafirs*, unbelievers. The building has since been beautifully restored.

As in the old days, the concept of Iran is vague and flexible, and the Persian (sometimes Dari) speaking elite stretched from Ottoman Istanbul to Mughal Delhi. Iran often and still does consider its cultural area to be larger than its current borders. The Shahbanu and Shah offered, in the 1970s, to pay to rebuild some of these Herati complexes, to restore some of the former glory to the city. They had the money and the expertise, since they had been restoring buildings since the 1930s.

Well, Afghan pride being what it was and is, the offer was proudly rejected. They would never accept Iranian help—they would do it themselves. They would restore it "better than." Of course nothing materialized; only a little cement was slapped on here and there. Cement that actually caused damage as it did not mix well with the ancient mortar. Ironically the Pashtuns who dominated the government, who made this decision, had never been involved in building any of old Herat. No one asked the Heratis. Many Afghans viewed Iranians as sissies, "opium addicts." Afghans grew it but rarely used it; they exported it. They thought that Iranian wealth was unfair—"They got it through oil; they didn't work for it."

In the summer the wind blew for 120 days, hot, dry. They would put brush in bundles in front of their windows, pour water over it: a swamp cooler. Others had *bad girs*—towers with openings that funneled the breezes down below over an underground reservoir, cooling the air. They had vertical windmills, masts with four matted panels—the wind would hit the panels and the masts would rotate, turning the millstones, grinding the grains.

There were dark rugs woven in the area, some with hooked concentric diamond designs. Except for perhaps a touch of white in the borders, all was indigo, dark blue, green, blackish. It just seemed dark at first view. Only with time, as the eyes adjusted, did patterns, intricate lines and colors, emerge. Some colors, such as blues, stood out best in night lights or by the moon—they had almost a metallic gleam. These rugs were noted as "night rugs" and valued for this. Some kilims, flat weaves, were also very dark and intricate. The light was strong and sometimes harsh. Perhaps the dark hues provided relief, but then the Turkomans in the north used almost only reds and their light was similar, and other groups, as in Iran, preferred vivid hues. The Baluchi preferred dark and browns. Cultural responses to similar environments?

In recent years the Ishmaili Agha Khan has been very involved in the restoration of buildings in Herat. No one else was doing this. The citadel has been massively restored and shrines and gardens will now last a few more centuries. What the new rulers will do is unknown.

## ๛ 45 ๛

# Karim and Healing with Snakes

O nce I rented a house in an old village on the edge of Kabul. The village was originally separate from the city, but now Shahre Naw (New City) touched one side of it. It basically was a hill covered with flat-roofed adobe homes. Maybe it was a "tell," with layers of villages built upon layers of the remains of older villages. Perhaps there was some Buddhist monastery, or fort, under it all, I don't know. I once was told that the last foreigner to live there was in Mughal times (the 1600s).

Down the road there was a women's garden, a place where veiled women could go and be unveiled. It was high walled, and by the trees rising above these walls, it appeared to be the usual *bagh*, garden: alleys of trees with sunken squares or rectangles filled with fruit trees and flowers beneath. But since I could not go in, it remained a mystery. It also seemed to be abandoned.

A large swath had been bulldozed on one side of the village through houses and fields and was to be a new direct route to the northern highway. But at that time it was just bare earth and dust. The village was to the right, homes and fields to the left, and further down the dirt road to the north, there were slight glimpses of the palatial white British Embassy and English cottages set in massed trees, then hills and the Hindu Kush mountains.

In a mud wall facing this barren path was a wooden door opening to a bridge across an irrigation canal, then a huge old mulberry tree and an irrigable flat yard to the right. On the left was a path up some ten feet of slope to a house—with a separate small room and outhouse to the right. There were high walls, with roofs of the village to the back and trees in the deserted garden to the right.

It was a simple, newer house, but I liked it because of the location and the water (so unusual). I bought two pairs of wild ducks in the bazaar.

One day, a few months later, some friends were over and noticed a small snake. Afghans really don't like snakes. They hate them. They took over, killed it, and put it under a large rock outside the garden door. We were on our way to a picnic and they said it would probably not be there when we got back. I said, "It's dead!" But they said the snake had power. Hours later when we returned, it was gone. I said, "Okay, something got under and ate it." They said it was the power of the snake.

In the next few days, I noticed more snakes, mostly in the unplastered adobe brick walls, or near the top of them, where pieces of slate topped the walls and where baby birds were hatching.

I was uneasy. I didn't know what kind of snakes they were—didn't know if this was natural or whether, as some said, the villagers put them there to get the horagi, foreigner, out. The villagers were friendly but . . . .

One day coming home from work I saw my house worker, standing, waiting for me outside the walls. He said he saw six different kinds of snakes and didn't want to go back in.

The only person I could think of who could help was Agha. So I sent a note with my house worker asking for his assistance. Of course I understood that he felt it would be unseemly for him to come over, so back came a note saying the only thing I could do would be to call Karim Morgh-yeer; Karim the snake catcher.

So some Afghan friends went to him. And back came my friends and a short man in gleaming white *perani tobans*, baggy pants and shirt, white turban, and reddish eyes, but he was not albino. He explained that Karim could not come but that he was Karim's assistant. We pointed out where the snakes were seen and asked him to get rid of them. He asked for some empty cans with lids and then asked me, because I was a foreigner, to stay in the house. I don't know how to explain this, but I intuitively agreed that my energy and my vibes were different and could be sensed, so I happily watched from my doorway.

He then went to each area and located the snakes in the walls, under a slate or deep between adobe bricks or in the rafters of the outhouse. He spoke to each one, and one by one they came partially out to where he could take it and put each in a container. He collected six or so snakes.

When he was done, he came towards me with a can and asked me if I wanted them. I said No, please take them if you want. He did want them and was very pleased. He did not do this jokingly. We paid him his fee and a gift. I then asked him if he could do something to keep them away.

"Bali", yes, he said, and asked for some sand. He held it in both hands and moved them up and down praying over it. Then he scattered it in the areas next to the walls and places where he found the snakes. Interestingly we saw no other snakes in those areas. But there were snakes in other places, so I moved.

Later I learned that the small whitish snake that came out of the rafters in the outhouse was a krait—they fall on their prey, bite, and death comes very quickly. I should explain that Karim's helper wanted the snakes because they were used in healing.

A week or so later, I went to Karim's shop. I often went to unusual situations with another horagi, foreigner, feeling partially that it was safer, but more so, that I would have a witness—someone to discuss, and validate to others, what we had seen.

So B. and I went down towards the old city, by the mosque and shrine of the warrior who fought with two swords while headless. This is near a very ancient Hindu Temple to the mother earth Goddess, Asmai, at the base of Asmai Hill. This temple has reportedly been at the same site since the people were Hindu.

Traditional shops were like garages, closed with wooden shutters, elevated two or three feet above the ground, so that a merchant could sit and talk to a customer who would be passing by. Modern shops were, of course, on the ground floor.

We found Karim seated amidst numerous boxes, many round like hatboxes, and bottles of herbs, and who knows what. We saw a crowd of people in front of his shop. Being taller, we could see over most—there was a young man with paralysis in his left arm. He was standing facing Karim, who was seated.

Karim pushed back the left sleeve of the man's shirt, put some dried leaves in his mouth and chewed them. With his left hand, he moved his thumb to each finger as if he were counting something. He picked up a knife with his right hand, and blade down, moved it down to the arm and then down the man's arm to his wrist several times. His hand was firm, and I expected the skin to break and bleed, but it did not. After several scrapings, the knife was put down, the counting stopped. He took out the substance he had been chewing, it was purplish, and gave it to the man to put in his mouth, which he did. Then he slowly opened a round box and took out an exquisite silver and black banded miniature cobra. Maybe it was a baby, I don't know, but I do know that it was extremely beautiful—like an exquisite piece of jewelry. The almost glowing metallic beauty was in stark contrast to the quiet organic tan adobe walls, weathered brown wood and muted colors of the clothes people wore.

The crowd moved back, we all moved back quickly, leaving the man alone before Karim. As I said, Afghans, like most of us, are usually terrified of snakes. But the man stood where he was, and Karim touched the snake all over the man's arm.

After a few minutes, he put it away, back in the box, and the man began to move his arm. The crowd murmured and began to leave. We came up and I introduced myself and explained that I was the horagi who had had the snake problem. He was very happy to meet us, thanked me sincerely for the snakes, and invited us to his house for lunch or tea—he wanted to show us his "big one," cupping his hand about a foot apart, and emphasizing that it was a big one and he was happy and proud of her. He explained that he used all these creatures for healing and seemed very open about it all. Not very brave around snakes, especially huge ones, I very politely declined.

Clearly Karim and his ways dated back to pre-Islamic times, to when they were Buddhist or were Hindu—perhaps related to Naga snake stories from India and probably much older than this.

In the opening shots of Kabul in the movie *The Horsemen*, you can catch sight of Karim the snake catcher.

What happened to him? Anyone like Karim, and there were unusual healers in many places, was banned or killed under the Taliban as un-Islamic. The first Taliban government media tersely reported that Karim "had died."

Later I learned that the mother of a family I knew, an educated professional, was ill and having exhausted medical help in India and Europe turned to Karim. They had predicted her passing soon. After working with him she lived a few more years. He was respected as a very kind gifted healer by many.

## ❧ 46 ❧

# A Head, Food

J amal, an government archeologist, dealt with foreign experts and was a frequent visitor to their homes and functions, and shared in their lives when on archeological digs. But he returned to a very humble home. So to bridge these two worlds he did what others did: he tried to capitalize on his expertise in his field.

One day I was invited to dinner at the home of Al K., a member of the American Embassy. As I entered I was surprised to see Jamal there, the only other guest. He seemed both happy and embarrassed to see me. After dinner I learned why. From his briefcase he sheepishly took out a somewhat round object about a foot across, wrapped in pieces of cloth. As he unwound layer upon layer of material, you could see gray stone. From this bundle of rags came a very beautiful head of Buddha, in the Gandharan style. Buddha, a tribal prince from present day Nepal, was portrayed in classical Greek sculptural form.

This style prevailed in eastern Afghanistan and northern Pakistan beginning under the Kushan emperor Kanishka (A.D. 130). In an attempt to find a human representation of the Buddha, a marriage was formed of Indian art and the Greek art that remained from the time of the conquests of Alexander the Great around 329 B.C. Greek art continued in the area, especially north of the Hindu Kush in Bactria. Buddhism has been in the area since the time of the great Indian Mauryan emperor and missionary Ashoka (268–233

B.C.). His stone-carved edicts, also in Greek and Aramaic (the language of Jesus) scattered throughout the subcontinent proclaimed his beliefs, also tell of his sending missionaries as far as Syria, thus perhaps influencing even people such as the Essenes of the Dead Sea Scrolls. The land is filled with reminders of the rich East-West contacts.

This head was exquisite, finely carved, in perfect condition. The gray stone, schist, was a favorite medium, as were terra cotta and stucco. The eyes especially brought focus to a face of transcending calm. "All is well," it seemed to say. "All will be well." Jamal explained that the head was all that remained of the statue, that it was from Hadda, near Jalalabad.

This was a major pilgrimage site. Old Chinese reports tell of its former magnificence. With over one hundred stupas, it was also noted for its stucco depictions of realistic underwater scenes. Major archeological work was done here, and the site had reconstructed and protected educational displays. All this was literally bulldozed by the Taliban.

The head, as was obvious, was an exceptional piece, and he wanted $500 U.S. for it. He also explained that he did not sell pieces. This was an exception; he desperately needed money. Clearly embarrassed, he added that due to his position with the government he was jeopardizing his entire career, his life.

Al, the host was a bit taken aback by all this. It was clear that this business was not what he had intended when he had invited Jamal to dinner. He explained that he had religious and ethical values that prevented him from getting involved in illegal deals. He also had his position in the diplomatic corps, which prohibited such transactions.

Modern crafts and rugs, he enjoyed purchasing, but "antiquities" were strictly off limits. He explained all this calmly and kindly.

Jamal countered: But they—diplomatic and foreign workers—
all do it. The Europeans are the worst, always trying to get something for nothing. They ship all these things out through the diplomatic pouch," the private, secure mail service available to embassy
staff. And the U.N.! Antiquities were valuable, people greedy.

Due to diplomatic procedures, nothing could be done by Afghan authorities to stop this cultural bleeding. Then, of course, not
all Afghans were interested in preserving their cultural treasures.
Various businessmen and individuals in the government and the
royal family were involved in the business.

The story goes that over two thousand heads were uncovered
in Hadda and sent to the Kabul Museum. It was said that whenever
the king had an important visitor, or a visitor he liked, he would
have his private secretary phone the museum and a head of suffi-
cient importance would be sent to the Dilkusha (heart captivating)
Palace. The king would then bestow this head on the important
diplomat or visitor. They would be allowed to take it out of the
country. Everyone said, and Jamal confirmed, that there were few
"heads" left. His Majesty was generous. But the heads were free,
whereas if he had given new rugs or lapis lazuli, he would have had
to pay for them out of his own pocket.

Later the host explained that another reason some stayed away
from "old things," besides ethics, was that some who bought were
later blackmailed by the sellers before they had a chance to deposit
them in the diplomatic pouch.

At the time I felt that old things, antiquities, belonged to their
respective countries and should stay in that country. Once I was
soundly lectured by a well-educated Afghan friend who said she
agreed with my position but then emphatically added, "Do you
think most people here appreciate these things? They sell them,
they break them, they shoot at them. (Following the religious rule

of no images faces were destroyed.) These things should be in places where people value them." I argued with her then.

Since then countless sites have been destroyed, the Kabul Museum was first plundered by the Soviets—no one seems sure of what was taken to Moscow—then the partisan shelling of the area, then ruin by the Wahhabi-Pakistani sponsored Taliban, the Bamiyan Buddhas blown up by the Taliban using Chechen experts (whose own historic sites were destroyed in their Russian wars), pieces sold in Pakistan, all other so-called un-Islamic sites destroyed, and on and on. Miraculously one brave Museum worker hid many treasures that later were taken on a world tour. But the Taliban have returned.

During the severe drought and famine of the early 1970s, sites were occasionally dug up so that artifacts could be sold to buy food.

One story was about a town in the east that was suffering during the 1970's drought. The villagers knew that there were sites nearby, but they had felt that these places should be left, respected; the past, the dead, their ancestors, should be left alone. And diggings might unleash spirits, jinns. Besides, the government had set a policy, not always adhered to, that looting sites was a severe offense. And there were cases of individuals and even whole villages being punished according to the new laws. But hunger and looming death caused this village to convene a council of the elders. They debated and reached a decision. Since they had exhausted their resources, and refused to sell their children, they had only one thing to fall back on—what their ancestors had left in the ground. The people were sworn to secrecy, a group of young men were given the task of going to the site and digging at night. They went by dimmed lantern light and had instructions to refill the holes by daybreak so as to not arouse suspicion. They dug down, artifacts were found, some were selected and taken, and others left. They did not take everything they could have. The holes were carefully refilled, all marks of their presence erased, and the remainder of the site left untouched. There was no greed in their actions, only honest need. They explained that they took only the number of pieces that they felt would bring enough to buy the food they would need to see the village through the famine. The rest was to remain there in respect, and possibly in case they were ever in such dire straits again.

These days it is a big business. Tragically, recent excavations of an astounding Buddhist monastery are threatened by a short time line because the Chinese Government has purchased the mineral rights to the copper beneath it.

# A Picture of Nur's Grandfather

One afternoon Nur Agha showed me a photo. He pointed and said, "This is my grandfather!" (His grandfather had taken his part of the Qadiri Sufi/Darvish ruling family out of British controlled Iraq and moved to Afghanistan.) The photo was one of the strangest I have ever seen. In some shops there were wondrous old photos for sale from Afghanistan, Pakistan, and India. Some were of stern-faced warriors, decadent aristocrats, or kings dressed in clothes and finery no longer seen. Of course photos of women were rare. They were not to be seen. These photos were like frozen fragments of a world now gone. Compared to the uniformity of most modern dress, they could have come from another planet. If the man had wealth or power, he had to exhibit it: gold and jewels on earrings, necklaces, decorated daggers, and rifles. Frozen eyes, cruel eyes, antimony eyes, huge beards, and strange, sculptured mustaches. Their looks reflected ways of thinking and values alien to us now. Show your wealth, intimidate those below you, advertise your power, your fierceness, your remoteness from others. There was never a smile.

I had seen many of these photos. Looking at them made the history I had read come alive. I could believe the stories of treachery and massacres and torture and needless "death before dishonor."

Photos of the British Raj showed lives lived, sacrificed, "for the sake of King and Empire"—rigid, set lives; rigid, set faces. Those of Indian princes reflected the greenhouse culture of generations upon generations of caste and privilege, of tremendous wealth, and often tremendous corruption and waste. The Afghan photos reflected fierce tribal patterns. One had to look proud because of one's father or tribal lineage. Or one had to look imperial to keep the clan or tribe in line: if they feared you there was less chance of rebellion. Or the face simply reflected the cruelty he had inflicted upon others or that had been inflicted upon him. The old photos also told you of the rug designs, of buildings and landscapes that have changed so much.

These pictures were strange and wonderful. But this photo was stranger by far than any I had ever seen. It was a window onto a very different and strange place. It was a Jeshin photo. Jeshin is Independence Day. And on this day the Afghan king sits and reviews his troops, as thousands watch. And everyone celebrates their final victory over British encroachment. The Afghans had three wars with them. The first, 1841–1843, resulted in a British evacuation from Kabul, wherein the story goes that one out of seventeen thousand survived. One pictures seventeen thousand British dead; actually most were from India. It was commanded by possibly the worst British general. The British retaliated. The second, 1878–1880, led to much destruction in Kabul. The third, 1919, was quickly ended by the British, who bombed Kabul from airplanes. The Afghans screamed, "Unfair! Fight like men!" It was brief because the British feared major sympathetic uprisings in Imperial India proper. Afghanistan was now recognized as independent. The king who led this brief war began a massive modernization program on par with what was going on in Turkey under Ataturk, and in Iran under Reza Shah Pahlavi. His wife appeared unveiled in the late 1920s.

All this change upset conservative elements and the British.

Who wanted a modernizing independent country next to a huge, wealthy imperial colony? Especially the "jewel in the crown" that was India. The eastern tribes, encouraged by the British, revolted with the help of a very conservative Sufi family. The king was deposed, and fled to Italy. A period of chaos followed with the rule of a Tajik, the first non-Pashtun ruler, a water carrier. His name was Bacheh Saqqaw, "boy or son of the servant who carries water in a goatskin." (Homes without wells had water brought to them in goatskins carried on a man's back.) He was overthrown by another branch of the former royal Mohammadzai clan led by Nadir Shah, who ruled for only a few years, 1929–1933, until he was assassinated by a student in the presence of his young son. This son, Zahir Shah, ruled from 1933 to 1973, when he was overthrown in a coup by his leftist cousin. This led to the leftist and the rightist conflicts of the next three decades.

Getting back to the photo. It showed a large tented pavilion from which dignitaries viewed the parading soldiers and groups. The king was Nadir Shah. In the photo only two people are seated: the king and Nur Agha's grandfather. It was a dark, tented structure, floor covered with good rugs, walls draped in dark cloth. There were numerous standing figures, some in military uniforms, others in various tribal dress, distinguished from one another by elaborate tribal turbans. Everyone standing had a stern, serious look as if ready, in case they might be given orders to perform some heroic or horrendous deed at a moment's notice. Old photos from around the world usually show stern-faced people, but this one was a few degrees sterner. The king, a thin middle-aged man, in military uniform, was full of self-importance and rigidity. The photo was an icon of Afghan power and fear—all except for Nur's grandfather. Seated next to the king, he was dressed in a light and dark patterned robe with a small turban. He sat, but not bolt upright in the chair like His Majesty.

He was leaning forward as if he were talking to the camera, as if he were a reporter on TV giving us the latest report of the parade. And instead of the uniform, frozen expressions, his face was dominated by a huge nose, and he was smiling, he was laughing, he was enjoying himself. Amidst the frozen faces and bodies he looked totally alive and free from their world. It was as if a photo of a modern man was spliced into this old military photo. He looked absolutely, totally out of place. He seemed as if he was talking to the camera and to future generations who would see this picture. "Look at these people and the crazy situation I am in. All this formality and fear, Isn't it strange and so silly?"

Nur Agha and I both joked about this. I asked, "What's he doing?" Nur Agha said he was laughing at the situation. "But why is he so completely different from everyone in the photo?" I asked. Nur Agha answered, "Because he was a real Sufi."

## ᚙ 48 ᚙ

# They and Them

O nce in a teahouse up north I overheard an elderly man talking of how "they" had come and had killed his relatives and had robbed and terrified everyone. He was bemoaning this and was sad. He went on and on, especially focusing on the cruelty. The others around him sympathized; everyone appeared to be very engrossed in it. They shook their heads and responded with the usual chorus of responses to stories. I was upset to hear this story and wondered if this had happened in the eastern areas, or between this group or that. There were numerous possibilities. He then dropped a name, "Oh, Genghis!" He had been talking about Genghis Khan and the Mongol invasions in the 1100s!

Sometimes when you would ask when some event had happened, you would get a vague reply. "In the past, in the past, I don't know, one hundred years ago, two hundred, many, many years ago." Near ancient ruins you could often find people who would tell you local versions of events associated with the site. "Oh, it was a great city, it stretched from here to way over there, it had . . . , it was . . . But then Alexander came and destroyed it." Alexander was not from 250 B.C. He was from the fabric of their lives. They knew the stories; they saw the ruins and the river. They lived in this history.

"Oh, Timur Lenk (Tamerlane) cut and destroyed our irrigation works. We once were wealthy, our family had . . . , we had . . . . , but now we are poor because of him." Timur attacked in the 1400s.

"Oh the English, they came and stole all the treasures in our country and left nothing, that is why we are so poor.

"Oh, the Arab armies came and fought with our people when we were Hindus. We defeated them many times but then they won and brought us Islam. But then they stayed and wanted to rule over us, they wanted us to be their servants so we fought with them. We defeated them and drove them out completely. They didn't like this."

"Oh, the Persians, the Irani, they are tricky, they say, 'Yes, yes,' but . . . you never know what they are really saying or meaning. They always wanted to control us. But they cannot fight like we can. But now they have all this money, they are rich. But it is not right, it is not fair, they have no right to it, it comes from oil, not from their work.

It's not right that they have money; we should have it."

"Oh, the Russians, the Soviets, they are godless and very bad."

Pakistan is usually viewed negatively. "They control land that should belong to Afghanistan—Pashtunistan, Punjab. The British took it from us and gave it to them. It was not right. They want to control us."

India, on the other hand, was viewed positively. They warred with Pakistan, defeated them. They had riches; it was warm. It all had belonged to Afghanistan in the past. "It was all ours before."

There was in the historical record and in the traditional stories the pattern that they, the Afghans, would come down from these mountains into "Hind." They would attack and pillage and come back home with riches, gold, jewels, and silks. This had been done over and over again for many centuries on large scales and on small scales.

"Hind" was a warm place, and a potential source of plunder, plus you could have "a good time" in the fight. It was also a good deed because they were "Kaffir", unbelievers.

Nowadays the blend of "past and now," "us and them" appears

to continue. The problems are because of "them"—"they" do this, why don't "they" help more, why don't "they" give more.

Depending on who you ask, Pakistan, the Arabs, Iran, Russia, the U.S.A., or someone else is to blame for meddling in Afghan affairs. And all the donor nations should give more, do more. All the woes have handy sources.

And then there is more local: "they" are stealing from us—the Pashtuns are . . . , the Uzbeks are . . . , the government families are . . . .

"They" are corrupt.

There is a great deal of truth in all of this—there always has been. But what is quietly missing from all this finger pointing is, say, the example of the Eritrean experience, a nation largely destroyed, not accepting foreign aid, rebuilding itself. Or all the examples of countries leveled by war but rebuilt even better.

Families exist, clans exist, tribes exist, and they fight to prosper.

But the "common good," the working together of a whole society—this has always been talked about, and very eloquently and beautifully. But when words need to move into action, the priorities of family, clan, and tribe always come first. So when people do work for the common good, it is often expropriated by others.

In the huge drug industry battle, a few fields may be destroyed to divert attention from important growers. Yes, the Taliban grew opium; then after they had stockpiled hoards and were feeling outside pressure, they banned the growing of poppies. And interestingly farmers complied, and more interestingly they did not starve.

Then you heard "If we ban poppies, the farmers will starve," so we must allow it! And huge sums of money are made—for this group or that. Is this money taxed, does the government profit? No, but families do. And some provinces are rich with the profits. And with this money you see their houses, traditional Afghan architecture and design, and gardens are ignored in favor of the loud, gaudy marble palaces in the worst Subcontinent style. And many of the well connected Afghans have large real estate investments in the Gulf States. And now the Taliban have again banned opium and focused on saffron.

Change this pattern? It is very difficult for an individual or small group to act independently if all their lives they have been raised not as individuals, valued for being unique, different, but as part of a group only? And they are not alone—in so much of the world, voting means supporting your clan, your tribe, your area, your political party. People need practice doing things individually. In fact in may places in the world people are not rewarded for individual initiative but are punished for doing things on their own, separately from their group. Anywhere in the world it is difficult to stand up to one's family.

# Polio?

Hamid was 21 or 22, from a middle-class family, where everyone worked and everyone needed to, just to keep going.

One day I heard that he was ill, very ill, and was unable to move much of his body. I couldn't believe it, at his age, but it was true. His family speculated that it was polio. "How could that be?" I asked. Surely he had had the vaccine! Yes, it was available, but somehow he had never taken it. Why? I asked. Oh, . . . they felt that it just was not necessary.

Now everyone was upset and bemoaned the fact that he had not been vaccinated for it. They were so upset and so sad that such a simple thing had not been done and now he was paralyzed and his life was ruined. He would be a huge drain on the family in the future. Their whole economic future was now much dimmer—what with doctor bills, and one less income to count on, his sisters might not be able to marry well, life would be harder, and they would have to take care of his useless body. This continued for about a week. Then suddenly, one day they said that he was better; in fact, he could move. It was not polio, the doctors decided, but some strange disease.

Strange diseases and illnesses were not that uncommon for the area.

I saw him, and he really was fine then. I said, "Well, you really are going to get your vaccines and shots, now, aren't you?"

"No, why should I? I am well." And the family agreed. No matter what argument I tried, I could not convince them. It was obvious to them that he was healthy now, so why do it.

Preventive measures are something odd to grasp for some. There were the foreign women nurses who traveled on horseback to remote villages to inoculate. They also tried to teach the value of washing hands and other areas of basic hygiene. Some people had always known such basics, but in rural areas life was different. They were resistant to some new ideas.

The village people would say, "*Bali, bali*, yes, yes, we will do it!" But everyone knew as soon as the horagis, foreigners, had left and things got back to normal, the old ways would return.

Of course strange, exotic diseases are more prevalent now, due to the fighting and poverty and the exploding population—so many children born to families who have very limited means. One can see news reports interviewing a long term refugee family, a man with 2 or 3 wives and 15+ children.

# ❦ 50 ❦

# Ghazni

Ghazni is a provincial capital city south of Kabul on the road to Kandahar. It is famous in the country as an example of what once was but is no more, the "Glory of Ghazni." You just had to say "Ghazni" and everyone knew what you meant. In its heyday it was the capital of the Turkish Ghaznavid Empire, which ruled and plundered across northern India in the eleventh and twelfth centuries A.D. Destroyed by the Ghurids, who built the mysterious Minaret of Jam, it never recovered.

There was a new city, and an old city on a rise next to the fort. Exquisite brickwork bases of several minarets, ruins of a palace, the tomb of Mahmud of Ghazni, the conqueror, a Timurid mausoleum, and further out the ruins of Buddhist stupas were all that was left. Foreigners were forbidden to climb the ramp or enter the old medieval city because of its proximity to the military base in the fort.

Now, during Ramadan, the month of fasting, people abstain from food and liquid all day. This is supposed to teach equality between rich and poor, among other things. It is to be a time of reflection; however, as humans often do, in those days many changed the nights of reflections into a fun happy time. People starved all day and overate and party at night. Anyhow, when darkness comes, everyone rushes home to their first meal, even soldiers. Ramadan, following the lunar calendar, came in winter that year.

So a friend, J. and I, dressed in our long winter coats, scarves, and hats took the opportunity to walk up to and try to enter the old city. There was a ramp up to the large gate set in the massive high adobe walls. We walked up to a man-made mesa. Layers and layers of buildings lay beneath—built, destroyed, and rebuilt because of its strategic location. We walked up and past the sentry. We passed as Afghans! Once inside, it seemed as if the very air changed. We were in a different world. The mud-plastered adobe walls absorbed sound; it was quiet. We walked down narrow, maze-like alleys, past small doors, large doors, very small doors, past steps that led to other narrow alleys, all of adobe: we were walking inside a huge earthen sculpture. It was dark and cold and silent and only the closed small doors offered a hope of entry into something different, into warmth and light. We turned right and left, not really sure of which way we were headed or had come from. The alleys narrowed, and we sometimes walked under overhanging rooms. I recall we hit a dead end and felt odd. It was like being at the wrong end of a maze and feeling that perhaps our luck was running out, and it was cold. We turned and slowly made our way out of that labyrinth. Past the guard, down the ramp, down into the new town and electric lights.

The Tomb of Abdu Razzaq, restored by the Italians, now an Islamic museum, was provincial Timurid, 1400s. Never finished, it is unplastered brick, shallow-domed, with no second, larger outer dome atop it for visual effect. These types of buildings were all prototypes of the ultimate masterpiece of Persian, Indian, Islamic, and Hindu design, the Taj Mahal. They are mandalas, Palladian, central domed, with sub-domes and rooms and passageways in perfect balance around.

I have seen many such buildings, but this one had a special touch of intimacy and earthiness. Its spaces were small—nook, cranny. The guardian of the tomb offered to show us the crypt. I thought it would be down some spiral stairway, but instead we went outside to the wall which surrounded the square property. We went to the right, to the middle of the northern side. There in the outer wall was set a small wooden door. He unlocked it. Following the flashlight, we stooped and made our way down and along a long corridor that led to a vaulted space below the central dome. In the darkness we could see further vaulted spaces of brick, but the floor was very dry earth. There on the dusty earthen floor were dark, large pieces of leather. He picked up one crumbly edge, uncovering skeletons. I never expected to see them just lying on the earth, covered with leather. It was not the custom, it felt improper, intruding; we left. Back in the sunshine, we felt free of something.

Hakim said his family was brought to Ghazni by Mahmud of Ghazni, and they had a scroll listing all the children, male only naturally, born to this family since this time. I asked him how they and the scroll survived the Mongol invasion in 1221 by Genghis Khan. The books are so clear about the massive destruction. "Well," he said, "the family lived a bit outside the city and nothing happened to them; they just changed leaders." Here, in a conversation, was a personal touch of the 1100s. No, not everything was destroyed by them. Many survived. Who else could have supported the Mongol Empire after the invasion and built their grand structures?

A Persian scholar once explained that the scribes for the Mongols were the survivors of the defeated peoples. Their world perished; they now worked for new overlords whom they despised. But they read and wrote, and they were the bureaucrats for the Mongols and they wrote the histories that have come down to us. We read their slant on history: that the Mongols were barbarians and destroyed everything. Yet a family lived a few miles away and survived and their scroll survived this "total destruction." So much for official history. History so often is "his history".

The ruins of the palace, the stupas also, and buildings have suffered.

## ☙ 51 ❧

# Leave and Never Come Back!

"If there is ever fighting in the city, gather your foreign friends and come here, it will be safe here." Nur Agha told me this several times, but I thought, "Things have been quiet here in Kabul since 1929." It was true that Afghans were always talking about possible trouble, tribal revolts, and revolution—that also reflected their flair for the dramatic. But one never knew.

Later, after the first coup, when the king was overthrown, I waited awhile before visiting Nur Agha because I was not sure of the political waters. When I eventually did go, he told me that several hundred armed tribal fighters had come in case his family needed protection. He said they did not need it, but that the men were reluctant to leave and that it was very expensive to feed them all.

Sometime after that I bicycled over to visit Nur as usual, late in the afternoon, after work. I saw a soldier posted at the outer gate. But I had seen them before and it had not been important. There was an outer gate, a courtyard and then another gate that opened into the garden and house. This time I smiled at the soldier, said *salaam*, and went into the first courtyard and told the tall servant that I was here to see Nur Agha. He looked very serious, left and did not return.

After a while one of Nur Agha's younger brothers came through the gate. He was well dressed in a suit and looked very serious, nervous and pale. He came straight to me and before I could say anything, he sternly said in loud very good clear English, "SMILE, act as if nothing is wrong, LEAVE, and NEVER come back!" He stared. I stared, said nothing, smiled, turned, and left.

As I slowly walked home, I experienced waves of fear and rejection. It brought back stories from childhood of people, family members in Ukraine disappearing suddenly into Nazi camps or the Soviet Gulag, stories of terror. The coup had put in power Daud Khan and leftists educated in the USSR. I wondered how my friendship with this family would impact them and me.

I left very upset, and wondered what was happening, why was I sent away, what would happen to me since their house was obviously watched and my visit was noted by the police.

Nothing happened to me, but months later I was told by mutual friends that it was safe to return. So I did. We were happy to see each other. Nur and his family said I had handled it well. They explained that in the morning of the day I had come, the Secret Police had come and told the family that they were in great danger. They were to pack their things and they would be placed in protective custody and taken to a safe, secure place. The Police would return late that afternoon, to get them, about the time I came.

The family decided that this was an elaborate ploy. They felt that the police wanted them to make some move. After all when the coup first happened many tribesmen rushed to this home to protect them. Would they call the armed tribesmen, provoke a revolt? Or would they try to escape the city? Then they could be charged with fleeing, thus proving that they were guilty. But they said they had nothing to hide, they were not going to run away. They packed some things and waited.

That's why they told me to leave. I had come late in the afternoon just when they were expecting the Secret Police to take them away. But the police never came, only me on my bicycle

# ை 52 ஒ

# Lonesome Doves

In the area north of the old center was Shahre Naw (the new city), commercial grid streets, and residential high-walled compounds of some small and some grand homes. One whole block was Shahre Naw Park, a large grassed oval encircled by deep channels and a walkway, with plots of trees and shrubs filling out the remainder of the block. On the north side was a modern cinema and a department store, but across the street was a piece of the "ever Afghan"—rows of simple mud kebab stalls. Small, dark rooms were entered past the trays of skewered meat that hung over beds of blazing charcoal, which smoked constantly from the dripping fat. The air heavy and dense with the smells of fat and burnt meat—the whole street was at times a cloud of smoke—and with radios blaring Hindi or Afghan tunes. At night the red of the fires, the dim smoke air, the smells, the music, and all the people totally blurred the distinction of modern and so old.

One day in late summer, I was passing the northeast area of the park and saw an unusual group of men seated on a raised earthen area under trees and bushes. These raised seating areas are called Takht, *Sofa*.

Several of these men I had seen before, wandering or seated, awaiting alms. I had never seen a group of them together. Some were "crazy" people, who in our terminology would be classified as mentally disturbed and thus probably medicated. But in these older parts of the world, people felt that, yes, some of these folks might be "crazy," or on the other hand they might be in touch by some form of the Divine, by some other reality. Not being sure, people usually treated them with some respect, and gave to them. There were malangs, men who were "on the edge"—perhaps crazed or perhaps aware of other spaces, levels of consciousness. Some used substances. Some people used the term *sadhu* for similar folk; this word comes from the subcontinent. A Sufi could be any person who was a sincere pilgrim in life looking for the deeper meanings in life; or a member of a specific order, with a teacher—a *sheikh*—and a set order of practices to do. Contrary to most Western beliefs, not all Sufis are open, loving, and embracing; some are conservative, and some are extremely conservative. Some Afghans say there are good Sufis and bad Sufis. Dervishes are full-time Sufis, belonging to more extreme orders, or to none at all. They are beggars, often with identifiable paraphernalia—a bowl, a hat—and are often "over the edge." Then there were the beggars: homeless, or professionals, or those with severe physical handicaps. There was the man who could not stand or walk. He was fitted with pads that were pieces of used tires over his knees; his hands held blocks of wood, and on these pads and blocks he would move across cement and mud and snow. Some, as in other countries, were purposely mutilated by their families in order to better gather donations.

Some had glazed eyes, possibly due to cataracts, which were prevalent in this high, bright, dusty desert light. Eye problems were common, and the largest Christian donation to the country was the Nur Eye Clinic, which helped the blind to see. It was highly respected and did not proselytize. But of course when the conservatives took over, it was immediately shut down. This also happened in Iran.

Some of these men sitting on their sofa in the park clearly saw something in their intense gaze; others seemed focused elsewhere and did not seem to see you. They were all together and yet they were all different from one another, and they all were different from the rest of us and were so treated.

This day, the six or so of them were quietly boiling water in an old kettle over a small wood fire—they used an old, stapled-together broken ceramic teapot and cups. They were having a tea party, gracefully slowly serving each other. Maybe it was the black tea that energized and refreshed the country, or perhaps it was the green tea that people favored for late afternoons. I don't know, but watching this group of men, perhaps "crazy" or touched by the holy, gracefully serving each other tea in their ragged, patched clothes, one could see or sense an energy, like the clarity of cold air, about them. Something was very different.

Knowing they might be hungry and not feel comfortable with a foreigner approaching them, at home I asked Ali, who helped with chores, if he could bring some *naan*, the large whole wheat flat bread, and offer it to them daily—discretely at this afternoon time. When he returned, he said they expressed happy gratitude for it. He was puzzled, but pleased they accepted. I—aware that I didn't and couldn't understand what they were doing—was deeply touched they accepted the bread offered. They met there in the late afternoon every day for several weeks; then I never saw any of them again.

# ꙥ 53 ꙥ

# Baluchi Chiefs

Late afternoon one fall day I bicycled over to Nur Agha's. I entered the first courtyard through the door next to the large double doors for cars and waited while a servant went into the house compound to tell him I was there and to inquire if I should go in. Nur said that when I came that I did not have to stop and wait by the gate but could walk through to the large house. But I felt it was better to show respect and wait to be admitted. Being allowed to walk through was very unusual in this country. Upon returning, the servant seemed a little edgy. He was very tall, maybe six feet seven, simple and dignified and respectful to all. He wore the usual baggy pants, sharewar, and long overshirt parane tomban with a long Western overcoat and dark turban.

He led me through the second set of gates. Usually I walked through the large garden area, with the shells of a couple of half finished homes in it, up the steps into one of the rooms in the large, simple white two-story stucco brick home. But today there seemed to be something happening in the garden. As I got closer, I saw a half circle of men seated on chairs under the trees. It looked unusual and important and I recall hoping that I would be led to the right, into the house. But as I got closer I saw that Nur Agha was seated in the center and that a chair was being brought for me to sit next to him. My heart sank; I would have to be on extra-careful, alert behavior. In such situations I was always anxious about acting inappropriately.

It was a group of men as I had never seen. Perhaps a dozen men, Baluchi by their appearance, middle-aged to senior, very, very dignified, aristocratic, with long beards—some gray, some white—clearly tribal elders. They were in gleaming white tombans, baggy pants, turbans, and extra-long *perans*, shirts, way below their knees. Some wore embroidered vests, and some exquisite gold or silver inlaid daggers.

As was the custom, they rose when Nur Agha rose to greet me. I shook his hand and then the hands of each chief. They were deferential to me because of my obvious relationship with Nur Agha. He introduced them as tribal leaders from the south, from Seistan, from Farah, and other places.

When we were seated, they resumed their conversation as tea was served. It was a formal, almost ritual talk. I remember I was very conscious of trying to do the right thing. I hated these situations. I knew had to be extra careful because anything I did wrong would reflect on my friends. And how could I know all the cultural curtsies and formalists?

One man spoke of how Muslim Afghanistan was. And everyone concurred and added Bismillahs, "Blessed be the name of G-d," and other traditional phrases in almost liturgical responses. Another spoke of how great this was and that all the people in Afghanistan were Muslim, all seventeen million of them. They all murmured agreement and seemed pleased. At this point Nur Agha seemed to dissent. The chiefs were startled, they didn't understand what was happening. And so one asked him how many of the people in the country were Muslim. Nur Agha paused for quite a while and said slowly he was not really sure. He repeated this several times and looked very preoccupied, as if he were trying to calculate, but was having a hard time. The attention focused on him intensified. All was quiet and I felt increasingly uncomfortable. I remember his fingers moving as if he were counting. Now the group, which was naturally focused on their meeting with him and quite formal, became very perplexed, agitated, and tense.

They knew the vast majority of the people were Muslims—Sunni, Shia, Ismaili, and others. Yes, there were some Hindus and Sikhs in the cities, and Jewish people, most of whom had gone to Israel but some of whom returned because they said life was less hectic and more comfortable here then. And of course there were small groups of various persuasions who kept to themselves.

The elders kept asking, We are all Muslims, aren't we? How many are there? The group was agitated. Nur Agha was quite calm and kept pondering something silently. He clearly knew what he was doing and was working the situation. I, on the other hand, was getting very nervous—I was the foreigner, the non-believer. "Face" was very important here, especially for the elders, who commanded instant respect in their communities, and here I was, a young outsider hearing a conversation I perhaps shouldn't. They were with one of their most respected religious leaders, a Sufi sheikh, a descendant of one of the greatest saints in Islam. Some viewed him as a living saint; some viewed the entire family this way.

Finally Nur Agha said he really was not sure how many Muslims there were. They countered they all were. He said, No, not really. They asked, How many? He said he really was not sure. They said, Tell us. Well, he said, he was not sure, but maybe there were four or five. Million? they asked, clearly horrified at his answer and that I was hearing this. No, no, he answered, four or five *nafar*, people!

They were shocked, and clearly stunned into silence. Slowly they asked what he meant; they looked very confused. *Ee tur ast*, It is this way: Islam teaches that education is paramount. Where are the schools for all boys and girls, where is the respect for women, where are all the universities, the hospitals, the help for the poor, the rule of law? He began to enumerate major concepts, but not the usual Five Pillars of Islam. Where is the love, the caring, the treatment of women, the . . . ? Who is living what they believe? As he went on and on, they were utterly silent. I was embarrassed and yet awed and silent at what had transpired.

One of them asked, What are all the others? Very calmly Nur Agha said, *khar*, donkey. It is a very bad word.

# ❧ 54 ❧

# Books, Problems with Thinking, and the Garden of Nimla

A s my friendship with Nur developed I began to do some research about Sufis and topics related to his world. I read all sorts of books on the subject. Some seemed to be almost a kind of science fiction, making everything mysterious and full of magic. They felt like they were written without a feel for the real life in countries of the area. Others were dry academic books, full of information but seemed divorced from everyday life. Then there were some that were a blend of both. I took one of these to him and began to ask him questions. Nur became curious about the book and author and asked to borrow it. He had difficulty with the English but said that he would get help. Some weeks later, with a big smile on his face, he gave back the book. He said he had a student of his, a language professor from the university, help him. They went through the book page by page. I was surprised by this thoroughness and asked what he thought of it. He had a very puzzled look on his face and said the book was confusing to him. He stated that about one third was correct. Another third was questionable, debatable material and that one's view depended on which Sufi group one belonged to. But he said over one third was completely off. He said he didn't understand where the author, a leader in the West of a large Sufi movement, got these ideas from. And actually the author claimed his family originally came from Aghanistan. He smiled and said of course this material made the movement more attractive to some, and certainly glorified the leader's family. I said if this is confusing to you how is a normal person supposed to get a real understanding of the subject. He answered that one always also had to have a teacher, a guide, someone who knew more than the person did and who was more developed and who had a clear sense of love about them.

This led to discussions about how people learn and see things. His views were identical to those I heard from Christian spiritual teachers I was familiar with. Namely, we talked about how basically a person is a very complex entity. And in various ages people developed skills and abilities in order to survive. No doubt when humans primarily hunted to survive their tracking skills, their hunting intuition skills were much more developed than now. These skills lessened as human life styles changed. At times when I lived in or visited various areas I was aware that in some areas people used their intuitions much more than in, say, western cities. In our high-tech world obviously linear thinking skills are paramount. Spending time around some tech people one becomes very aware of their specialization. Sometimes there also seems to be a certain lack of emotional connection. Laughter is a good reference point. One does not often hear hearty belly laughs with them or even with comedians on T.V. these days. The laughter is more restrained, cerebral. Sometimes cleverness, the odd connections, seems most valued in speech, look, fashion, and much of the modern art scene/business, conceptual, or graphic.

Nur stated, as so many teachers have before and since, that a person is much vaster than one or two areas, or the 4 Jungian areas—thinking, feeling, intuition, and sensation. In regards to books he said the authors usually used their thinking functions, this was also true for academic education, but other areas should be used and developed as well, he added. When I asked how many areas might a person have, he said something like twelve. He said that each had their value and all had to be developed and used in order to begin to understand life. He then said that few people did this.

He was very aware of Western debates about the existence of

God. He was puzzled as to why the spokesmen only emphasized their thinking functions in this debate. He laughed and said that this was like the ancient international story of the blind men trying to describe an elephant. Each knowing only what they experienced by touching one part, be it ear, trunk, etc.. He said if you only use your thinking you have only limited information and everything you perceive is limited by this one dimension. And he added if one did not value other functions then their input and information would not be included. But he said if one were open and tried to develop and explore and use all these many parts of oneself then, he said, a person could really begin to learn. I told him that many educated secular people would not accept these ideas. Yes, he said, he had seen this many times, and that people have very set views of life, fear of the unknown, of going beyond the usual everyday life, is a very strong human truth.

Then he added, don't you think that people 3,000 years ago thought they understood a great deal about life? Or people 2,000 years ago felt they knew so much more than people 3,000 years ago. And people 100 years ago felt that they were so superior to people in the past. And today with all our information and technology people are very proud of their accomplishments, and they should be. But there is danger here too he said. They, we, forget that life is so very vast. They, we, forget to remember that people in the near future will consider us, the people of our time, so uneducated. He said there is little humility, "reality" he called it, *perspective* is a word we might use. Fear seems to keep us limited in exploring.

As our conversation continued and changed I mentioned the garden of Nimla. I had recently visited there, and its strangeness had been on my mind. He laughed and said it fits with what we were talking about! It is located in a subtropical area framed by the White Mountains, or as people nowadays know them as the infamous Tora Bora of bin Laden fame.

Originally planted by the Moghuls of India in the 1600s it was typical of gardens of the area, walled with irrigated terraces in squared sunken plots, with raised treed walkways framing them. The plots, as usual, had fruit trees. Here pleasure mixed with practicality and a source of income. Under the orange trees were narcissus flowers, or sometimes vegetables. But here the alleys, usually lined with one kind of tree, had huge dark ancient cypresses, ever green, alternating with white *chinar* trees. These trees, similar to London plane trees or sycamores had white bark with vivid green leaves like a maple in summer, gold in fall. In winter ghostly white fingers contrasted against the dark cypresses. And all of this against the towering snowy White Mountains. ( the mountains were where Ben Ladin hid.)

The tree combination in winter was a great contrast. The normal calm of their green tree gardens was here altered as the eyes moved the focus, to the dark green cypresses, to the white chinars. And there were only two facets to focus on, both equal. People have so many more facets to use he said.

He emphasized that this garden was an image of what we were discussing. In the 1600s small young trees were planted, small, white bark trees with big green leaves next to the thin pointing pillars of a dark cypress. No doubt the plots were filled with flowers, and all looked new, young and fresh, happy and hopeful of a long future. A hundred years later the cypresses were tall and very dark green, in cloudy weather they were almost black. And between each of these was a tall chinar. And every inch of the bark a vivid white. When in leaf the green and white tree next to a dark cypress made a strong clear beautiful picture. The dark evergreens seem almost to be voids next to the white and green. Their darkness serves to draw the eye to the white green.

But these days the cypresses were huger and a somber dark green, still pointing to heaven. The irrigated plots were still planted with flowers and greens, and orange trees. And the white chinars were still white and their leaves green. But these trees, as they reach a great age, slowly start to shrink, to close in upon themselves as they age. They get shorter and more compact.

On the cloudy day in early spring when I visited the garden was empty. The plots were covered with narcissus about to bloom. The orange trees were green. The main walkways divided by a channel of water that fell in small waterfalls level to level were empty and the water channels were dry. These walkways led down ramps on either side of these waterfalls. And as in old gardens in Hind there were rows of niches in the wall behind the waterfalls. These were for oil lamps or candles to illuminate the garden at night. In the grand old Moghal gardens found in Pakistan and India all was of white marble with the lamps by night and vases of gold or silver flowers by day reflected the light from behind the carefully crafted sheet of falling water. There were niches too in the rounded pillars that marked the corners of the plots. Much larger pillars than these, very phallic in appearance, were used to count the miles along the roads in the Moghul Empire.

But this day there was no falling water, or oil lamps, no people, only wind and a cloudy sky, and a few cawing crows. Each cypress looked black, almost as if each was a huge pointed hole, a void. And on either side were the huge white trunks of the chinars that branched leafless up and outward, twisting and ending in thin elegant white fingers; white against the brooding gray sky and the near black of the evergreens. Nur said the range of appearances of the garden—from young and flowerful to mature, to great age, from winter to spring to summer to autumn, hot to cold—was a good metaphor for what a person could perceive and understand of life. A visit at a one given hour on one day in a given season, in a given year, be it 1620 or 1730, or 1890, or 1980, would give a person a vastly different experience. And if one were blind or handicapped in some way then this too would bear on what one experienced and perceived. What if one could smell the intoxicating flowers of the orange trees, or the overcoming acres of narcissus, or if a person was there when there was gleaming snow on the dark trees and white trees, or if one saw the ghost of the Moghul princess who is said to walk and hide behind the trees, or if one was there in its cool shade under a torrid hot summer day, or if one were sitting on beautiful carpets next to the flowing water and classical music was being played, or at night with the water and gardens subtly illuminated by oil lamps, or if there was a picnic . . . ?

A person could have vastly different experiences. Nur said that trying to "see" Nimla was a bit like trying to "see" the reality of life. One needed more than just cerebral thinking.

# ❦ 55 ❦

# Kuchi Wedding

One day a friend, a wonderful, bright young man, a son of a khan, came over and said to gather up some friends for that afternoon. We were going to a Kuchi wedding! Yes, things often happened suddenly there. Kuchis, also called Povindas, are proud nomadic Pashto speakers who traditionally migrated from high central areas of the country in summer to warm Pakistan in winter. Politics affected these patterns; they move less in those days. Kuchis looked down on settled people—farmers, town and city dwellers. They viewed them as imprisoned, as a sort of a degenerate version of what people were supposed to be.

I gathered some male friends and we shared a taxi to the southern outskirts of the city, where there were dirt roads, new walls and new houses, and little greenery. The student's house was simple but spacious, lots of windows upstairs, a place for their jeep, an outhouse, and a garden space that contained large sunken plots that were divided up into geometric flower beds. The family was an important eastern Pashtun family of great influence and wealth, but in tribal Pashtun fashion they lived simply and never flaunted it. The house was a total reflection of this approach to life.

We began walking uphill to the south, away from the houses, towards the mountain called Takht-e Rustam. Rustam was a figure from ancient Persian mythology—this was the *takht* or seat of Rustam. According to some, he performed epic acts in this area. But there were many, many places with such names.

The fields we walked through were mostly barren fields. The spring crop had been harvested. Off to one side were trees and the high adobe walls of a *qala*, a walled fort. The south side of Kabul and its mountains got smaller and smaller behind us. We passed a small walled compound and the numerous black goat-hair tents of the Kuchi. In one we watched a gray-bearded man shear a sheep surrounded by excited youngsters, who, though they had seen this done many times, were reacting as if it were their first. Excited probably because they were watching us watch them.

As we neared a group of tents, we heard drumming. There from a discreet distance we saw a circle of women dancing in their dark maroon and green robes, hair in tiny long black braids. Some were playing the *daira*, large drums in narrow frames, like huge tambourines. They were held aloft and turned into the circle and out as the women slowly danced in time to the beat, singing.

They were laughing and having a good time until they noticed us—they yelled. I was told they said it was a woman's place, men get out! By the men's red faces, I think it was ruder than that. So we continued on towards more drumming coming from further up the hill. There was a large group of men. Some men were seated under an open-sided tent; others stood speaking in groups. In the center were several men with huge wooden drums hung from their shoulders, which were beaten on both ends with sticks.

It was a deep, booming beat, compelling, very different from the complex higher timbre of the women's daira. Another man played a reed flute with a blaring nasal sound similar to an Indian *surnai*. Some men were doing the Atan, a national dance; others watched. Moving forward slowly in a circle counterclockwise, you leaned left and clapped your hand low into the circle, then you returned to a standing position for a beat or two and then leaned right, up out of the circle, and center, clap, then to the left again, and so on. The dance always started slow, and gradually increased in tempo, with turbans flying off, baggy clothes billowing, and the long hair of some tribesmen flowing in, then out of, the circle.

It was late afternoon when we arrived, and they had been danc-ing for some time. They continued into the night and more men came, stopped for the feast and some other activities and then con-tinued most of the night and the next days, and after we left.

We watched them as the sun set and the urban lights of Kabul twinkled down below in the distance. This contrast of where we were and the world of Kabul in the distance struck me again and again, that night and the next day and days later, during my normal life in the city. There were the electric lights of a modernizing city, but where we were—it could have been a thousand years ago: fires, drums, dancing, no sign of the modern at all.

It was hard to tell who was who in the group of men. The groom wore the basic perani tombans, pajama-like shirt and very baggy pants, that everyone else wore. His turban looked new, but so did other men's. The egalitarian tombans clothed everyone; only the cleanliness or the starch differed. But it was with their beards and turbans that men made efforts. Beards were always neatly groomed and sometimes hennaed.

Many men carried small round cases like a compact, for *nas war*, a tobacco mixture they'd place in their mouth for a time and then spit out. The rush you got from it depended on what your mix contained. These cases also contained mirrors inside their lids. You'd often see men—young, or old, gray-bearded men—checking their appearance, beard, turban, as some women check their lipstick and make-up in a compact.

Some of the men stood out for their turbans, which identified them by tribe, or for the attention they paid them. A chief was pointed out but he was indistinguishable from lesser men. Some stood out for details, such as a shirt collar or vest, which denoted Pakistani influence. But then, these were Kuchi, people who recognized no borders, who looked down on town dwellers and who moved and walked with a bearing that supported their beliefs. They were regal, proud and free.

This marriage was traditional, with gifts and dowries exchanged. Contracts and agreements were made. The ceremony itself was conducted simply with a mullah and a Qur'an in a black tent aside from most of the activities. People congratulated the groom when he returned to the men, as the dancing continued. More and more people arrived as if from nowhere.

Evening brought huge kettles of rice and meat and yogurt. We ate on rugs spread on the ground, Kabul glittering below and the stars above, while the drumming continued. Afterwards the dancing intensified. One man stood out, one legged with crutches; he danced and performed antics, sometimes dancing on his crutches. Suddenly other men joined our group, very friendly, with good English, Pakistani style.

Our hosts became alarmed and moved us on to another area.

"Why?" I asked. "Very dangerous men from Pakistan—murdered many." We moved on.

The drumming changed, and the now-huge circle gave way to theater. Men appeared in drag and skirts, and skits developed between the "women" and men. The men grew excited and found the antics hilarious. The crowd was roaring and every so often they would answer a short song with a boisterous chorus. The crowd was alive! I had not seen such mass excitement before; it had always seemed a country of quiet individuals. Here it was a mass of laughter, shouts, singing, and dancing.

The excitement intensified and our hosts seemed increasingly embarrassed that we were watching the drag show. So when they suggested we leave for sleep, I sensed that it was wise to go. We walked to the high-walled compound down the hillside. As we entered, the large wooden gate was barred, and we were led up to the earthen rooftop, up a ladder which was drawn up after us. There cushions and bedding had already been provided.

I then noticed that there were armed men on nearby roofs and on the roof of the corner towers of the qala. They stayed alert all night. Lying on this roof in the cool air I could see the lights of Kabul, the sky clear and alive with stars and shooting stars. I could hear the drumming and dancing, protected by armed men.

When I awoke the next morning, it was bright and clear and there was still drumming. Later, when we wandered up to the site, we found that many had gone, but it seemed as if they were still there, as if their ghosts were still dancing in time to the beat.

There still was a good-sized group dancing; some had danced all night. They were moving with great energy, and we could see that many were in an altered state. I wondered what it would be like to dance all night to the same beat, with your lifelong friends. It was not like some dance floor or disco, with anonymity, or even an ethnic party. Here you were dancing with your group, your tribe. It was part of a communal journey; you moved with people you were raised with, shared good and bad times with. You were really together.

As you walked up the mountains in summer and down the mountains in fall, year after year, it was collective, primordial. The people of the wedding were connected to our host by tribal and feudal ties. (*Feudal* is also a Persian/Dari word). Basically they were the khan's private army when he should need one.

In these days there are many fewer Kuchis; many have settled down, some in cities. Some are involved with the drug lords and warlords. Some still move with the seasons but they must fight with the farmers who increasingly take over their grazing lands. It is very hard for them.

That afternoon in the presence of the host, a Kuchi man asked about whether I was a khan (lord) or how I was tied to one in "Amrika." I tried to explain that our system was different, and said that I did not have one. He asked with some urgency, "What happens when you are in trouble, need protection?" Here he could always go to a khan for help. The khan had a lot of power and expected future reciprocity.

I was surprised by his directness and honesty in front of the khan's son. I tried to tone it down, but he stressed that the khan had all the power. One had to obey the khan's decision in situations. I knew that despite attempts to be polite, the gulf between his life and our system—which is very imperfect, as we are constantly complaining about—was so vast as to be almost incomprehensible to him. I explained that in my *watan*, country, people were independent and that we tried to work together to insure that everyone was protected and had the some rights.

"But how does it work?" he asked. I remember his urgency.

"We have problems, but we have laws, and people—everyone—has to obey the laws. It is not always perfect, but we really try." There was a silence. I said, "But you have laws here too."

"Yes, but the khan has power over the laws." He looked at me for what seemed to be a long time.

I didn't feel that he was scanning me to sense whether I was telling the truth. No, it felt as if he was trying to go inside me, to go into the world I came from, to taste it, to feel it. He then said gravely, Laws are good. Laws are very good. We need laws here."

## ❧ 56 ❧

# Nur's Teacher

I had been reading about Sufis and had seen the constantly repeated references to the rule that a person must have a teacher. They basically said, if you have only yourself, and no teacher, no matter what your intention, you only end up following pieces of yourself. You need someone outside of yourself to help you break out of the many little worlds we all construct for ourselves. I had never heard Nur Agha speak of his teacher and wondered who it was. Nur did have a high rank just because of his birth into this family. Would he then go to someone of lesser rank? How did this fit into the all-important social hierarchy of the country and religion? So the next time I saw him over tea, I asked him what he did about this requirement. Did he have a teacher here in Kabul?

"Yes, I have a real teacher."

"Who?"

"My grandfather!"

I was startled because I had seen a photo of him and knew he was not young back when it was taken in the 1930s, so he must have passed on. "How can he teach you? Isn't he dead?" I said.

"Yes, he's dead, but he comes to me at night and teaches me." Nur Agha laughed.

"He's dead and he teaches you?" I said.

"Yes, he is a great Sufi." He smiled at my perplexity.

# ❧ 57 ❧

# A Jinn

Jinn stories were common. Jinns, or "genies" as they are called in the West, are spirits that according to different sources could do various things, positive and negative, and could assume human forms. People had sometimes opposing explanations about what a jinn was and what a jinn could do.

Some attributed all bad events to the work of jinns and sought ways to purge them. Others said they could take possession of a person, and then special people would have to be called to exorcize them. Some even said that the dust devils, the miniature tornado shaped funnels that dashed across the desert floor were actually jinns. Others sought out jinns to help them in their careers, or love life.

The level of beliefs in jinns did not always correlate with the level of one's education. But then, people educated in precise sciences often become rigid in their beliefs. There is less space for unknown possibilities; things must be "exact." Ahmed, an educated man, an engineer, told me of his encounter with one. He was once alone walking in some large fields on his family's property, when unexpectedly he saw a young lady sitting under the nearby lone tree. Although at some distance from her, he could see her face. She was very beautiful and looked at him with deeply penetrating eyes. Stopping, he stood transfixed and felt his heart melting. He said he felt that he had suddenly fallen in love with her; it was love at first sight! He approached her, their eyes locked. But as he neared, he suddenly heard his younger brother calling after him from behind. Shaken from his focus on her, he briefly turned in the direction of the call. Then immediately turned back to the young lady, but she was not there. He ran to the tree, but no one was under or up in it. And since the tree stood alone in the large fields, he had a good clear view over the low growth of crops all around. He could see farther than anyone could have run in that moment he had turned. But he saw no one. He ran around, in various directions, looking for her, but saw only his brother approaching from the distance. And when he arrived, he too said he saw no one and had seen no one.

Ahmed said he grew more frantic and kept running and searching and calling out to her. His brother grew alarmed at his state and ran back to the home and summoned family members. They came running and trying to calm Ahmed, and joined in the search. Then they tried to console him and gradually coaxed him back to the house. But Ahmed was feverish in his recounting of the story and in his great desire to find her. No one could calm him down; he ceased his normal life, stopped work, and was obsessed only with her.

Then his grandmother took over. She decided that the "young lady" had been some sort of jinn. She had prayers said, drew out her amulets, and prepared herbal remedies. Under her care he gradually calmed and eventually was able to regain his normal life.

## ✍ 58 ✌

# Shirin Gul

Shirin Gul, Sweet Flower, was the name of a gracious lady whom it was my privilege to know. From a good, old family, well educated, she was raised partly in India. And because her family was large and scattered, she had traveled. Perhaps it was a touch of India, but I think it had more to do with her soul; there was always a sparkle about her—her eyes, a look, a gesture. It was always this way, even when she was dealing with unpleasantness; there was always this sparkling light behind whatever her everyday self had to do. She had an executive position in a large company.

Increasingly women worked outside then, wherever they could. It was not easy; they constantly had to prove their worth to the male dominated world, and had to deal with endless put-downs. They almost all wore scarves, babushkas, in quiet colors draped gracefully over their heads. These women did not cover their hair completely. They covered more or less hair depending on the given situation. They would judge where they were, who they were in contact with, and would quickly adjust how much hair they would show. This was all a sort of a version of the white scarf all the school girls had to wear. Shirin Gul had hers, in various shades and used them with more than the usual, wonderful grace of Afghan women.

And when she had to deal with serious things she did so with equal grace and authority, but then always used her secret weapon to strengthen her point—her beautiful, magical smile. This look,

filled with her great love of life, flowed from her. This smile sparkled with the same light as her eyes. They were more than bright,
they were alive with life.

She greatly valued her family and friends and had a great, open
heart for anyone in need. Known for her charity—she was always
searching for ways to help others whose lives were harder, to develop, to better themselves; and there were so many!—she was
more interested in teaching others how to fish than to give them
a fish.

When you met these kinds of women, who had emerged from
layers of restrictions, who did so much, you could not but wish
that they ran the country. Their strength, courage, practicality, and
compassion—you were sure—would thrust the land into a new day.

Many times she gently explained the ways one lived in this
country to me. When one is in a new, unknown land and feels loved
by such a wise, knowledgeable person, then, as I did, you feel protected. She was a great host. I have no dramatic story about her
that I could tell you, but I could list for pages upon pages the many
simple kindnesses that she extended to others and me. She was like
a gentle rain upon dried earth.

At the beginning when I was setting up house she inquired what
I had bought, what I had done. Of course she could not visit—that
would not look good, people would notice, and there would be social repercussions. Nodding as I told her of my purchases, she said,
"Good, good." Later that day her servant brought over a bundle
wrapped in cloth that he said was on loan to me, for my house, as
long as I was in country. I asked him to convey my thanks to her
and went inside. Too heavy and small to be a pot of delicious food,
I gently unwrapped it. What could it be? I wondered; she was a very
practical person. But it was a small, simple model of a building in
India made of white marble. I recall just standing there looking at
it, speechless.

My room then consisted of two long cotton cushions on the floor, Afghan style, to sit and sleep on, a printed cloth on a wall, curtains to help keep warmth in during the bitter winters and then to help block out heat during the hot summers, a small rug, and a low wooden table to eat from, to write on. I put the model building on the low table—and it suddenly became the center of the room. Coming in, or sitting, eyes always gravitated to its whiteness. It was a delight. When next I saw her, I thanked her profusely. Her eyes just sparkled as I spoke.

Then she simply said, "You needed something beautiful in your place." Only then did I realize how true it was. Just like in the story of the Taj, beauty transforms. She added that it was a going-away present given by some Hindu friends in India, that it meant a great deal to her, and that when I left, I would please return it to her. Of course I did.

As I write this, I realize now more than ever, that here was wisdom and an extraordinary lady. Another time, when I first moved into the house where I had to call the snake catcher, she asked me to consider something. I said, "Sure," then, "What is it?"

Families who could afford it had servants. It was an encouraged way to help employ people, and it was also necessary, as a wealthy or educated person could not be seen cleaning, washing, or doing other menial tasks; this would be scandalous. Different people did different levels of work—this is true in much of the world. The Western idea of shared chores, getting your hands dirty, is anathema to much of the world.

Often whole families would be servants to another family, children doing errands, women housework, men outside. This continued for generations sometimes. There would be modest pay but mostly free housing, food, and gifts on holidays, such as a new set of clothes. Servant kids and the boss's kids were often close but when school time came, life divided them. The family children went to schools, the servant children did not. Only in stories did one hear of a servant raised up and treated equally. Of course, too, in Kabul most of the servants were Hazara Shia, a discriminated-against minority, and so the ethnic and religious divide stepped in.

Well, Shirin Gul's servant family had just had a young relative come down out of the Hazarajat, the central mountainous area of the country. He needed work; I needed a servant. I said OK. Then she added that Ali needed to be taught how to cook and clean, and so on.

She said her servants' family would help teach him. "Good," I said, then realized her grand plan. He would be taught how to work in an Afghan home, but if he was to have a "better" future, then he would have to learn how to cook and clean for foreigners. She had found an opportunity for him to better himself. So I said I'd find another servant to teach him how to do all these things. She looked and smiled; her sparkling eyes said, "Good, you caught on."

When I was about to leave the country, she and her family invited a friend and me over for a farewell dinner. This was a surprise to me since I had not been there for a while. The father had wished to advance his government career and it was better that foreigners not be around the house. I understood and just accepted it as part of the reality, just too as when I saw certain people walking down the street, we would not greet each other. It would have led to rumors and gossip if we were noticed doing so by certain other people. It was understood; I understood that this was the way. So I was surprised and pleased to go when I was invited.

The food was wonderful as usual, Afghan with a touch of India. During the dinner the father took out his *tasbeh*, prayer beads. Men often took them out, fingered them, praying or just using them to relieve tension. Strands with ninety-nine beads represent the ninety nine names of God. They can also have thirty-three or eleven beads or any multiples of eleven, or any odd number. You finger a bead and recite a name such as al Rahman, the Almighty, al-Rahim, the Compassionate, and so on. Some beads were of stone or wood or even plastic; the value depended on the person's pocketbook. His were of dark reddish carnelian. This was the favorite stone and color in the country for men. He explained that it had taken him years to assemble these beads. He had chosen each to match the whole. They were beautiful.

He was seated at one end of the table; I was to his left. He held them out for me to see and hold. Then said he wanted to apologize to me. I was shocked; saving face was an important element of the culture, especially for men and especially for men of his position. The others at the table were surprised also. I said there was nothing to apologize for. No, he said, there was: he had been wrong and he wanted to say so. He explained, "I kept people like you away from my home because I felt it would help advance my career. It did not. And I chose that over spending time with honest people like yourself. I was wrong and I apologize." I said I understood the situation and there was no reason for this. He ignored what I said, as was his custom.

"Please accept this tasbeh as a token from me." I was shocked again. I couldn't possibly accept such a gift. "Please you must, I can't, please . . . ." Then the voice of Shirn Gul and others entered in and stressed that I must. It was only proper to do so. Reluctantly I did. But I was overwhelmed. There were always big surprises here; what you thought you knew of the people and the culture could quickly be overturned, and you would be left with a feeling of being very, very ignorant.

After dinner, during tea, Shirin Gul said she had a gift for me from the family. I didn't know what to expect, but I knew from stories that other friends of theirs, years past, had been given old Khyber rifles. They were not a wealthy family but, as is customary with Afghans, they were very generous; more generous than most.

She handed me a package and said that I must accept it. Given the arguments over accepting the prayer beads, she repeatedly stressed that I must accept. I didn't answer yet, fearing what it could be. I was told to open it. As I did so, I saw it was a heavy textile. It was silk but very heavy, almost like a canvas. It had brightly matching stripes; it was gorgeous, possibly a veil or a wall hanging. Only a master weaver could have combined the vivid colors in such an exquisite way. I said, "This is so beautiful, but it's old. I cannot accept such a gift."

"Take it!" she said. She explained that it had been in her family since the early 1800s.

"It's an heirloom," I said. "I couldn't take this."

The argument went on and on. But there was a determined look in her eye, and something else. It was a look from some deeper part of her soul. And it said, Trust me, take this, you will see. It was this deep look that spoke to me, and I did what she directed.

At the end of the evening as we were saying our goodbyes, I shook hands. I shook hands and kissed the father on both cheeks, as men do there, and as I was shaking hands with Shirin Gul—one does not kiss a woman in Afghanistan unless family—I leaned over and kissed her on the cheek. I was surprised at my action and expected a negative reaction from her. But she was not surprised. The deep "trust me" look in her eyes was there as it said,

"Yes, this is right."

A year and a half later I was working in Iran. One day my supervisor, Semeen, a woman who epitomized the grace of Persia, handed me my mail with a letter that had come from Afghanistan. She gave me an odd, concerned look as if she sensed something. The letter was from one of Shirin Gul's daughters. I opened it and read that Shirin Gul had been ill and was taken to the excellent medical facilities in New Delhi, India, but it had been to no avail. I froze and Semeen, noticing that something was wrong, came over and comforted me.

Later in Kabul, Daud Khan, who had overthrown his cousin the king, was replaced by the leftists, and then they were replaced by another leftist and the Soviets. Life was reduced to war.

Shirin Gul's daughter, in nomad disguise, bravely risked all to smuggle herself and her young daughter out of the country. And her father, sedated, was locked in a box as cargo in the back of a truck. They made it out of the hands of the Soviet-led government.

When I heard that they were safe in the United States, I offered to send back the veil. The daughter insisted that she would not accept it even though they had had to abandon almost everything in Kabul when they had fled. We argued and argued. Finally we found a way—she could not accept the return of the gift to herself, but she would accept the return of the gift on behalf of her daughter.

I also returned the tasbeh. The heirlooms were back in the family.

I think that "trust me" look allowed me to be a bridge. I had the veil and beads for a time; now they were back with their rightful owners.

I was her vehicle. It was good to be a vehicle.

## ᔄ 59 ᔅ

# Azziz

One day, before some friends asked me how old I thought Azziz was, I could sense that they were up to something, but all I could do was to go along. They perceived that I realized this, which just increased their pleasure and mischievousness. Being mischievous and witty was a constant in the country. Making someone laugh or scoring a point was valued. And, sometimes, total absurdity was greatly appreciated. Laughter was laughter, but it was also a cultural response. The old adage "laugh or cry" was true, but here laughter was preferred.

As people said, this was a reaction to the harshness of life. Sometimes what sounds like laughter is not laughter.

A vivid event: once, high-ranking Afghans were invited to the USIS (United States Information Service), to view a documentary on the assassination of President Kennedy, who was well known there and very popular. Also in the audience were Americans from USAID (United States Agency for International Development), the embassy, and other programs. Now, most of these people and similar-ranking personnel from other countries are not particularly aware of the culture around them. They mostly live in large houses, have chauffeured cars, socialize mostly with themselves or other expats from various countries or the Afghan elite.

These foreigners live very comfortable lives, are highly paid, and often get spoiled and addicted to this semi-grandiose lifestyle. So the audience was composed of comfortable Americans, other comfortable foreigners, and comfortable Afghans, all comfortable with one another and all sharing great sympathy for the documentary's story. Well, the film began and went on, and at the point where the president was shot—the Americans braced and were moved—many Afghans began making sounds that sounded like a quiet sort of laughing ! The Americans were absolutely horrified and outraged— laughing at the murder of President Kennedy! People shouted at the Afghans, who in turn were shocked that they were being yelled at with such rage. It was a disaster, but after the dust settled both sides managed to learn a little more about each other's culture. The Afghans were horrified at the assassination and responded in one of their ways to release tension, a way they had developed to deal with death and all-too-common tragedy. They sort of laughed but not really. This sound can be very cultural. Many cultures respond to bad news with a kind of laugh, others view it as mocking.

So, that day the students laughingly asked me to guess Azziz's age; a handsome, slightly stocky young man with black, slightly curly hair.

I'm not good at such guessing, but thought late twenties would be safe. The group laughed knowingly and congratulated themselves for my answer. When the frivolity was over they got back at me. I then asked him, and he said something in the late thirties. I was shocked,

"No!" "Bali, bali, yes, yes," they chuckled and went into further "I told you so" and "of course they don't know," and so on. Then someone stated that Azziz was a "charsee." They then began to try to explain this situation simplistically so that the horagi, foreigner, could get it.

*Chars* is hashish—a concentrated form of marijuana. It was a major reason so many tourists came there. They smoked it, or ate it, got high on it, and basically used it for pleasure. Though some, part of the more serious hippie strain, used it to explore themselves and spirituality. It was available in lumps or small greenish patties, or bricks; and there were many, many stories about its manufacture and uses.

Some said that boys ran and walked shirtless through the marijuana plants and that the oils collected on their skins was then rubbed off and pressed into the dark greenish solid bricks. Some Afghans use it or marijuana, but generally not other drugs. True, they grow opium, which they sell to Pakistan, Iran, India, anyone. But they look down on its use. Opium was not proper; it was for weaklings, for "them" not "us."

Now Azziz smoked hashish, this I knew, but . . . . They explained that this was not just smoking as most people did. He used it in a very serious way. And yes, he looked much younger than he was, certainly full of energy and was more alert than normal. These features and more were due to his practices. They said that the results were clear, but that they felt the process was too much for them. He had a guru-like teacher to whom he owed loyalty. He was instructed and taught, as he was able to hear.

Azziz belonged to a group, a sect with a set system which had to be followed. It was loosely termed a kind of Sufi group, but clearly had ancient pre-Islamic roots. One had to obtain the chars from the group, and it was not just any chars. It was a special brand, grown and nurtured and processed in a certain way. It could not be brought, and was available only through the teacher. It had to be smoked at certain times of the day only; certain dietary restrictions applied. And overall a set life pattern had to be followed. Azziz chose this way and clearly he had some very observable results. He told me that he was happy with this but that it was not always easy. He didn't divulge many details and curiously he didn't have the aura of a devotee or sense of "love you" that others on other paths have. He seemed to be a regular guy, a bit more intense and somewhat to himself. A year or so after I left that job, I ran into him by a rug store. He seemed exactly the same.

There were many chars groups. They were accepted as part of normal life, but were not always highly respected. And there were many, many stories.

Once I was told of a man's visit to a group up north of the Hindu Kush, in a special compound and garden. There was a secluded dimly lit room, which was decorated on the exterior and interior with sheep horns, antlers, ibex horns, and so on—pre-Islamic customs. There was a high, carpeted platform on which the group sat on red rugs and a special brand was smoked through a tall hookah, a water pipe. The person reported that it was very strong. Some chanting was done and after some time suddenly a few took out horns and reed instruments and began to blow deafening sounds. The visitor reported that he was terrified, ran out, and left the city. He was uncomfortable even discussing this.

A friend who was very involved in this culture told me his experience. As he was known to his friends as one who "smoked," but was also curious about deeper levels, he was invited to join a special group for an evening. They traveled out of Kabul to the huge valley to the north, just over the hills.

From this valley, a Silk Road center, one can go east and join the road to Jalalabad and India, and west to the Bamiyan Buddha valley and then on north or west to Iran, or north into the Hindu Kush mountains, up the Salang Valley to the tunnel at 11,200 feet built by the Soviets to go onto northern Afghanistan and Central Asia and beyond. Or up the extremely narrow gorge where the road is cut into the cliff above the raging glacial Panj Sher (Five Lions) River. This opens up into the beautiful valley made famous for being unconquered despite five massive attacks by the Soviet war machine.

These defenses were all masterminded by the legendary leader Ahmad Shah Masoud. His later assassination was the signal use by Bin Ladin to launch the 9/11 attacks. There were Buddhist stupa ruins in various valleys, and in the center of the vast valley are the ruins of Kapisa, one of the Alexandrias of Alexander the Great, and later the capital of the Kushans, site of a major archeological find of the 1900s: Roman, India, Syrian, and other artifacts of the riches of the Silk Road. The southern half of this valley was destroyed by the Pashtun Taliban, it was stripped of all vegetation, orchards, and vines, because the local Persian speakers resisted them.

Well, my friend and this group went down various rural roads—graded gravel with flanking irrigation ditches with pollarded mulberry trees—past fields, orchards and walled compounds. They came to a gate to a large walled garden. The double doors were massive. Usually in one side of such doors is a smaller inset door, used for everyday, a door in a door. They entered and he described a large walled orchard-like garden, with its rectangular sunken areas holding fruit trees and flowers beneath. But this garden was more meticulously kept than the normal. Every detail was attended to, and the flower beds were elegantly composed and gorgeous. Deep into this heightened environment was an adobe building, of one room, carefully plastered. Inside was a raised platform, carpeted, and alongside was a water pipe some six feet, two meters, high.

The group assembled and began their rituals, prayers, and then smoking the special brand of chars. Again this was a very special group; they were using the substance to draw closer to God. It was deeply serious and yet not overly pious, but kind and warm. The newcomer was not a stranger to drug use, and had used just about everything. He said he inhaled from the hookah and was soon very, very affected. Almost immediately he was in a much-altered consciousness. He said simply that it was stronger than any LSD he had ever tried, that it was a very sobering experience and he would never do this again, ever! It was too strong for him.

Now, of course, all these groups, if not eliminated by the Taliban, are very careful about people knowing of their existence.

## ↢ 60 ↣

# Sarwary

One day wandering in the old city, in Shor Bazaar in Kabul, I saw a man. He was a smallish man, in pants, shirt, and suit jacket—there was a certain upright dignity about him, and under his arm he carried a board and what seemed to be a large, what we would call Persian, miniature-style painting on it. I had never seen anything like it there before. I greeted him and started a conversation with him. He was from the western city of Herat, had trained under the renowned traditional miniaturists in residence there. With limited horizons there, he now lived here, worked for the government at the usual low wage, and was trying to sell his work with little success. I asked to see what he was carrying—it was fairly large and was an enlargement of a miniature scene. The style was that of Behzad, fifteenth century, Herat, the time of Timurid culture. His version was balanced, vigorous, and much simplified.

It was a hunting scene, men on elegant horses racing after antelope or ibex in an idealized mountain landscape. Of course there was the water, a stream with a large waterfall, and strange trees, twisted and huge, and strange mountains with peak after jagged peak. Each flower, each tree was striking in its clarity and boldness, as if each was a portrait only of itself.

An art historian once wrote that the vividness of these old miniature paintings was akin to looking at a flower at night with the high-beam lights of a car directly focused on it. This made sense—because the colors and form stood out, it was more than realistic. But then perhaps this historian had never experienced a high altitude desert where the air is thinner and the light is glaringly bright, where people use various means to protect their eyes. And, too, perhaps he had not been in a landscape barren of green—the opposite of lushness—where browns and tan and grays stretch to the horizons. To see a single bright-colored flower in this seeming desolation is like seeing it under spotlights.

The same effect could be had when one was walking, especially on a hot day in the adobe mazes of a town, where there were only the browns of the dust at one's feet, and the brown walls, and the brown weathered wooden doors and the intense blue skies. And then suddenly a door might be ajar, or someone might leave a compound. And you just caught a glimpse of a few flowers in pots or a single green tree or perhaps a lush walled garden. The monotones and then a flash of color—it might be a potted geranium, but it was for a moment all the colors of paradise, all under a spotlight.

His name was Sarwary. Yes, he could do real miniatures, but it was very costly—materials, natural ground pigments, gold leaf—and labor intensive. He was having a hard enough time attempting to sell these larger, much cheaper versions.

We went to his house for tea, simple brick, two rooms, no glass in the windows. He supported his wife and mother, very nice, friendly, open people. They lived on the slope on the other side of the mountain the old city banked into.

As in many countries the rich lived on the flat land, where walking was easier and water could be obtained by deeper and deeper wells, and there was soil to have a garden. After all, farmland was limited and valuable. The poor lived on the rocky hillsides, up steep paths made of rocks, covered with ice and snow in winter, windswept. Their simple adobe and rock houses, often precariously perched, offered breathtaking views of the maze of the city, of the stretch of city and beyond, of mountain ranges after mountain ranges. It was beautiful, but water was carried up in goatskin bags on the backs of carriers, and sewage was hard to have carried out. And it was all hard.

The ancient Bala Hissar fortress, blown up by the British, was to the east and from it, up and along the top of this steep mountain ridge, ran a wall. Originally built as a city wall to protect the Hindu city from Muslim attack, it had been maintained off and on since.

A story goes that a ruthless king ordered the people of the city to build it, men, women, and children. If one died working, or was too weak, the person was simply added to, embedded in, the wall. Bones were visible. One day a woman could no longer stand it, refused to work, and everyone, though exhausted and terrified of the king, joined her in revolt. He was killed. Happier days came. Again, as in the battle with the British at Maiwand, it was a woman who turned the tide.

It was clear that Sarwary had talent, was poor, and needed help. I bought from him, showed the work to others; many bought, shops began to carry him. I asked him to paint a scene of a Sufi sitting on a rug, writing, with the major sights of Kabul in the background.

Now when I look at it, it appears to be me, writing this book, ironic and fitting. He prospered some, bought glass for the windows of his house, bought better paints and materials.

I don't know what happened to him after I left. But years later in a bookstore I saw a new picture book on Afghan and Pakistani decorated trucks. In this part of the world they are often brightly painted and lavishly decorated with fanciful scenes, the Swiss Alps, the Eiffel Tower, the Taj Mahal, the tropics, paradise. Often postcards from far-flung parts of the world were used as inspiration and then modified to fit local taste.

It was wartime so the photos were taken in Pakistan. Some of the fantasy scenes looked vaguely familiar, and when I looked carefully at the bottom of the scenic panel, I could make out the name Sarwary.

## ❧ 61 ❧

# Famine

There was the custom that once a month the U.S. Ambassador's home would be open to the American community. Lots of good food was served. All levels of people came. The USAID had rank; the lowly Peace Corps volunteers did not.

However, this changed abruptly when word of the drought and famine became official. Prior to this, people were urged not to talk about it—you might be sent out of the country. We Peace Corp were told to avoid anything political, like talking about the famine , or we would be terminated. Now USAID became involved; The U.S. donated wheat. Part of massive surpluses at home would be distributed in a "wheat for work program." But U.S. law stipulated that there had to be an American presence when it was distributed. Employing USAID personnel would be very costly and problematic. Peace Corps volunteers were viewed as a simple answer to this problem. Early twenty-something American young men fresh out of college would go with wheat shipments, check on the wheat for work projects, oversee distribution, and try to minimize corruption. They were flexible, willing to rough it in very remote areas, eager to learn, naïve, and relatively invisible. They were a cheap American presence: the Embassy and the Peace Corps were pleased. The Ambassador was friendlier.

There were many stories about the corruption. Here you had a desperate situation, food worth a fortune, and ancient patterns of patronage and corruption. People had centuries of experience in bribing, hiding, looking the other way—they had to. It is a very old pattern. It is a world wide problem.

There were projects in areas not affected by drought but inhabited by Pashtuns, the ruling ethnic group. Sometimes different ethnic groups were paid at different rates. And of course there were some people who actually thought they knew what was going on, only to find out the bitter truth. But it must be remembered that no matter what, huge amounts of food did get distributed and many, many lives were saved. So, perhaps it all could be viewed as a diplomat in a capital might view it, in the long run . . . . There were also stories about the people hurt.

In one valley in the western highlands there were two tribes living next to a river. One group relied only on dry farming, winter snows and rains providing for the harvest. The other group diverted water from the stream to irrigate their terraced fields. As the snows and rains did not come, the first group's crops failed—they sold off their rugs, jewelry, valuables, and children, and began to starve. They did not irrigate, it was not "the way" of their people. The second group irrigated and though the stream shrank, there still was water enough to get some crops harvested. They were surviving.

Another village was found in a destitute condition. They were approaching starvation. But there still was some water in their stream and some deep pools where fish had gathered to survive. When questioned why they did not eat the fish, they replied that it was against their religion. When Muslim leaders explained to them that this was not so, they refused to believe it. They did not eat them.

Animals had to be slaughtered in a ritual way, their throats slit. The meat has to be halal, similar to kosher. As the drought continued, animals just died. Religious leaders told the people that if they found an animal that had just died, it was permissible—due to these extraordinary days, after all life is precious—to eat the meat. Many people refused, refused to adapt, to eat unclean meat.

To outsiders this seemed ridiculous, stupid, and insane. Why die? Yet for them, faced with the increasing likelihood of their own death in the near future, many felt that violating ancient family, clan, tribal, and semi-religious restrictions was simply not a good idea. It was temporary relief with possible eternal ramifications— not a good investment!

I recall watching the irrigation canal that ran through my yard get lower and lower day by day until there was no water in it at all. I kept thinking they just need to put other water into the system; gradually it began to sink in that there was no other system.

One day I was coming home and saw some kids tending a herd of goats, a common scene. However, I stopped and watched. Skinny goats were up in the old, low mulberry trees; the leaves had turned yellow and brown. The goat was high on a branch desperately straining, trying to reach and bite off leaves to eat. The boy and girl had sticks and were hitting branches trying to knock down more leaves for their poor animals. There was nothing else for the animals to eat. I remember feeling scared. This was a scene of desperation.

In the massive drought of the early 1970s, possibly up to five hundred thousand died in the ensuing famine, and the pattern repeated itself in the late 1990s, during the Saudi- and Pakistani-supported Taliban regime. Their response to the famine was to announce to the people that this was because they were not praying correctly. If they prayed properly, then under their distorted view of Islam, all would be provided for by Allah. Aid organizations had to adopt all sorts of strategies to get the Taliban to even allow relief supplies in. Now the Taliban beliefs have returned,

These days the snows and rains have been less; no doubt the loss of trees and vegetation has been a factor. And the population has increased so much!

# ❧ 62 ❧

# Nuristan UFO?

One day I was having tea with Abdul, one of Nur Agha's brothers. He said he wanted to tell me about something that had just happened. He was intrigued by it and wanted to know what I thought. It was late winter and Nur Agha was still in Jalalabad, a subtropical area on the route to the Khyber Pass and Pakistan. Many city people or their families escaped there for the winter—school was out because it was too expensive to heat them. It was an area surrounded by snowcapped peaks. Horribly hot in summer, it was springlike during winter months.

The very rugged high forested mountains of Nuristan were to the north, and a delegation had come from an area there to see

Nur Agha. Now, they were recent, forced, converts to Islam. King Abdul Rahman had declared jihad, holy war, on them in the 1890s. Facing the choice of death or conversion, they acquiesced and became Muslim. However not all surrendered, a group fled to the British side and were welcomed. They continue to keep their fascinating very ancient religion. They are known today as the Kalash people.

As recent converts the Nuristanis are very scrupulous in religious matters and have their own unique cultures. They are very honest, and in speaking to Nur Agha, a religious figure of importance to them, they certainly would not lie. Now they came to him because of something that had recently happened to two members of their community.

They didn't know what to make of it, so they came all the way down from their high villages on icy trails, then mud ones, on foot, then miles over semi-existent roads to seek his counsel and his explanation of this event.

Now I should explain that in those days when I was there many rural people were not aware of issues or topics of interest common to the world media. Yes, people had radios but if they didn't speak a major language, they could only enjoy the music. Many people were unaware of popular, controversial, or cult trends in the world.

Some weeks previous, two of the men had gone out hunting on a clear, cold day. It was winter and though their village had provisions, dried foods, milk, and grains, they were eager for some fresh game. They had to walk through deep snow in the forests and up and down the endless ridges. It was later in the day and they were about to start back home when they emerged from the forest into a small clearing on a ridge. They froze at what they saw, and being hunters quickly hid themselves.

They reported that they became very scared as they began to comprehend what had shocked them so. The clearing was on a ridge with snow about two to three feet deep. It was a very cold, cloudless day, with the usual bright blue winter skies of high, dry altitudes, gleaming snow, and dark forests. In the middle of this small snow-covered meadow was a large, silver disc-shaped object. It gleamed like metal in the intense light. It was bigger than one of their wooden houses.

They had never seen anything like it. They came from a land of mountain peaks, trees, wooden houses, and cotton and woolen clothes. Most of what they needed was homemade and home-grown. Here was a huge, smooth object. It was not a house, or a vehicle like a truck, which they had seen in the lowlands. And it was here in their area, and there was no road for it to have driven up. They stayed concealed and watched it. After some time, a panel in the object opened and two human-like beings emerged. One of the Nuristanis, in fear, raised his rifle to shoot. The other man pushed the gun down and quietly but desperately urged his friend not to fire. They didn't know if those beings were good or bad or danger-ous, and what weapons did they have? His friend agreed and they stayed in their positions, very, very scared.

The two beings were not tall and were covered in a silver col-ored suit of some odd material. They walked through the snow a bit and then returned to their craft, and the panel closed. After some more time the craft rose slowly straight up and then sped away very rapidly. The men were stunned. Gradually they got their courage up and went over to the site. There was deep snow everywhere but exactly where the craft had been, there was none, just the ground. But the ground was not wet from melting snow. It was very dry. There was just a patch of dry meadow where "it" had been and then two to three feet of snow. And the snow at the sides of the space was not melted or damaged by intense heat. It was just deep snow, and then no snow—dry meadow. The men were very alarmed. This did not fit in with their experiences of the world, no snow, no melting, a flying metallic disc, silver people.

They returned to their village, told of their experiences, and, being honest people, were believed. But no one knew what to do: should they mount guards, prepare for attack? And no one knew how to explain this experience. Of course, they had stories of seeing unusual things flying and some of them had seen them for themselves. But never had they heard of such an encounter. Village asked village but no one had an adequate explanation. Was it the government, or jinns, spirits, or another country, or what? So they braved the muddy, slippery trails and set off for the towns and schools far away in the lowlands to find someone who knew what they had seen. They asked but received no adequate answers and were sometimes laughed at, though most people, knowing of their honesty and seeing their expressions and earnestness, only shook their heads and said, "I don't know . . . ." Then they continued on, and went to Nur Agha.

He listened to their report of their experience and said that he too knew little of this. Except to say that the beings that they saw were divided into two groups, there were good ones and there were bad ones. It was good that the man did not shoot, for it is best to stay away. Abdul said that he had heard stories from other countries about UFOs and flying saucers and aliens. He didn't know if they really existed. He asked me what I thought.

To me the universe is so vast that to think we are the only intelligent life form seems to me to be the height of human narcissism and hubris. But I didn't know. I had read and heard stories. Some seemed credible and others seemed to be fantasy.

I told him that after a severe snowstorm when I was growing up, all airports and roads were closed. Suddenly, people in the street quietly shoveling snow looked up, pointed, and started to ask "What are those?" We all saw several silver cigar-shaped craft move rapidly across the blue sky. There was a strange silence, no one said any more, only us kids speculated.

Abdul said, "You know those Nuristanis are very honest and direct.

And they would never, ever lie to Nur Agha." We just looked at each other in silence for a while; then as everyone does, changed the subject.

## ❧ 63 ☙

# Dancing , The Guys Talk

We were warned not to go because of the likelihood of violence, but also because our bosses seemed embarrassed or afraid.

Periodically a large tent would be set up on the edge of a town. And at night lights were lit and it would be filled with men who came to watch the "dancing boys." (Actually they were teenagers. *Bacha* could mean boy, or servant, or sexual partner, or any subordinate). Of course because women were treated differently and could never dance in public so the only recourse was to have men do the dancing. Logical.

A stage would be set up. An orchestra of a few traditional instruments—a harmonium, a hand organ, a rebab, a drum—and a singer were the minimum required. They would set themselves up on the makeshift stage and begin warming up.

A form of music called Logari, coming originally from Logar province, is common. This is traditional peppy dance music with a stimulating beat that suddenly stops in the most unexpected places. When the music stops, you stop dancing. You freeze in the position you are in. If you move or continue dancing, everyone laughs at you or you might be disqualified from dancing, a sort of dancing musical chairs. You begin dancing only when the music resumes. This music is not just for dancing boys, it is also common at most parties.

Here at these dancing boy tents, it is often used. A young man comes out dressed either in gleaming white or light colored perani tombans, the usual baggy pants and long shirt, or in beautiful women's clothes. Since is was all popular in Pakistan also, many cultural influences came from there. They might wear the gold embroidered slippers with up-turned toes that one saw in the bazaar. Their eyes might be made up with antimony, and their face with other make-up. This is the stage after all!

The music would begin and one bacha would dance very seductively to the all-male audience. Now the thing to remember is that the audience is not composed of what most people would picture as a stereotypical gay audience. No, these are regular guys, married with children, tribesmen, warriors used to fighting, especially during the past decades of war. They are tough men, often armed, but in the presence of a dancing boy's seductive gestures, all changes. Yes, they appreciate good dancing but they really enjoy the allure. The boys move about, on tiptoe, gesturing, eyeing, but the moment the music stops they freeze, usually in a seductive way. This charges the audience up. The music resumes and then stops again, then resumes, stops, raising the tension in the tent. Some men become very impassioned as their hearts fall for a particular dancer. Men compete for the attention of a dancer—money, usually in small denominations—is thrown at the dancers, who continue on. Gifts and money are spread liberally to musicians too.

Because one never knew what to expect, we were told to keep away. Among Westernized, educated people this was all sometimes a source of some embarrassment that men would be so drawn to young men. But ordinary men and women would laugh and say, "Oh yes, yes, the dancing boys!" They think it's perfectly natural that men should behave in such ways. The men were all married after all and all the really old cultures of the world had similar arrangements. They recognized the range of human experiences.

Another custom, popular especially in Kandahar, seems to have a clear connection to ancient Greece. A man, married with wife and children at home—of course in these areas the wife is never seen and even to ask about her is very bad form—well, here, a man is free to have an *ashna*, a younger male lover, who is showered with gifts and status. The man is free to be seen in public with his lover, to even parade him around to arouse others' jealously. Of course the younger one now has a reputation of being the passive one. As in many cultures, if a man were viewed as the passive one, the "woman," he had a great stigma attached to him. This also reflects their very negative view of women, but this attitude exists in all "macho" societies. But as he matures, marries, he regains his status and can take a young male lover too. This custom existed despite the common view of Sharia, Quranic law, which condemns homosexuals to death.

Under the Taliban men they suspected of homosexuality were buried up to their necks and a heavy wall was collapsed on them. If they were still alive when dug out, they could be hospitalized. Often without supplies, these institutions could do little.

Sex overall was not something openly discussed. All this was framed by Persian language poetry. The biggest problem limiting discussion of it was the fact that almost all of the vocabulary pertaining to the parts of the body and their functions could not be discussed in "polite company." So either one used gross "street" words, or one used poetic expressions that were lovely but vague. The flower of the morning, gate, the root, and so on are not terms that can readily be applied when discussing family planning, or venereal diseases.

Even in the family husband and wife often refer to each other in poetic terms, the sweet bird, the flower of the morning, the flower of the pomegranate, my lion.

Rahman, a neighbor, was young and curious about Westerners'

sexual habits. The common assumptions are that Westerners have almost no values and have sex all the time with just anyone. How else could one explain how a family would allow their daughter to travel alone to a distant land unescorted by family, or all these young men traveling but unmarried (at their age!), and all of them wear such revealing clothes! Of course Western movies just reinforced these notions, along with the idea that all Americans lived in huge houses with unlimited amounts of cars and other expensive things. He was curious, just as I was curious about their customs, so we would exchange stories and information.

Religious laws, tribal laws, lack of privacy, being constantly surrounded by others, the segregation of the sexes, all contributed to very little boy-girl contact. Yes, children played together, but then at a certain age they were separated, except for family members. There was no dating, no coeducational activities, and schools are segregated by sex. So what do young men do when females are so distant? Yes, as in all "old cultures" around the world, young men do have contact with members of the same sex.

He told me that when possible, guys would try to have sex with servant girls or with female cousins. Of course they were very careful to protect the girl's virginity, so the "back side" was used. Of course, too, the servant girls were less important. But this was all not so easy because there was so little privacy. Men were free to associate with men, so sex was sought this way.

"Of course," he said, "I have had lots of bachas. I do it to them. No, they do not do it to me. Yes, I was in love with Karim, and he loved me too, and we had good times, but then my heart changed." Then I told Rahman what another friend, Abdul, had said—that "all" the young boys have it done to them by either friends, or relatives, uncles, older cousins, that the younger ones have no choice, the others are older, have power, are stronger. Abdul refused to talk about his own experiences. He just kept repeating "all."

Rahman tensed up at what I had related and then said, "No, that's what he says. We do not do this, it is against the religion. He is a liar, not me! I am not a *koonee*, I am not one of those!" In this macho society, as in most countries from Latin America to Africa, to be the dominant one is not bad, but to be the receiver, the "woman," this is disgraceful. There were stories of men who had committed suicide because it became publicly known that they were "the woman." Sadly, this also gives a clear picture of what women are thought of in these many places. They did not like to discuss oral sex.

Daud explained to me what many others had also explained, that in Dari, the older form of Persian used in the country as a lingua franca, as well as in modern Persian, the pronoun for "she" and for "he" is the same. So when one reads the great love poets of the language, be it Hafez, or Firdawsi, or Rumi, or any of the many others, one is not sure if the "beloved" referred to by the author is a man or a woman or if it is a reference to God. He laughed when I said that all the Western translations I had seen of, say, Rumi, were to a woman. "Are you stupid?" he asked. "There was Rumi, and there was Shams: two men, no women! Women are good, but why do they write that?"

I said people are not comfortable talking about such things. He added that they have this problem too, that in Islam all this is bad, *haram*, so we don't talk about this. It is not polite. He said they use beautiful words, poetic words that are like a cover to what people really mean to say. "Even my mother and father do not call each other by name; they call each other things like 'jewel' or 'bright eyes,' or whatever they think of at that time. It is beautiful!"

"Yes," I said, "it sounds very romantic." And this has been going on for millennia, I thought. Here on the one side, all you see are restrictions, yet if you just look a tiny bit deeper you find ancient ways people have developed to deal with their needs for physical contact, for tenderness, for love. In what looks like rigidity you find a comfort with a wide array of ways of living.

One day on a picnic (these are very popular there), all male. I was struck by something that amazed me and sort of shocked me by its creativity and gentleness. We were all tired after eating and some of us found the trunk of the only tree and sat leaning back against it. Zahir and Hamid were without anything to support their backs, so Zahir told Hamid to sit up and then he sat with his back leaning against Hamid's back and they chatted. So extremely practical. I remember staring. It was such a simple solution to a basic human problem yet I had never seen two men do this in my country. It would have seemed inappropriate somehow. It was crazy. Here these friends were more comfortable with their bodies and with touching, at least same-sexwise, than in any Western, "modern" land.

The influences of the rigid Islamic fundamentalists have taken a toll on openness, and people are careful.

## ∽ 64 ⋳

# Tourists

In those days, hundreds of thousands of tourists passed through the country—many Europeans—German, French, English—and many Americans.

There were wealthy tourists who stayed at the Intercontinental Hotel, up on the saddle above the Baghe Bala Restaurant—this building still stands and still hosts visitors. There were various moderate hotels available, and then there were the cheap places to stay, modern buildings or former homes. These catered to what were generally called WTs (world travelers), people overlanding from Europe to India and beyond. Some came for adventure or history. They had read books, heard stories that had struck a chord in them, so they came.

Others came for the drugs, mostly hashish, and were on their way to India, Nepal for the really good "stuff". They were en route, yet also enjoyed the country and the substances.

Usually they'd follow the road, west to east, enter through Herat, then go to Kabul south via Kandahar. Some would leave Kabul to go up to Bamiyan to see the Buddhas. A few would journey north of the Hindu Kush to Mazar-e Sharif to see the blue-tiled shrine and the white pigeons, only white, at the shrine. Some would stay in Kabul quite a while. Most were sincere folk, but some, lured by their drug trips, would get lost in that world.

There were stories, like the world traveler who died and whose friends sought to send the body home. After lengthy proceedings, someone at the airport customs got suspicious and had the sealed coffin opened. Inside—no body, but bags of high-grade drugs. The friends had buried the body in the garden of the home they were renting and tried to make a lot of money smuggling.

There were deaths and there were mental breakdowns. You'd see WTs, post hippies, really high, sometimes the women dressed in flimsy, revealing clothes. This in a conservative country was a total invitation for trouble.

As usual, the Embassies did not like to get involved with their nationals, preferring to be diplomats.

There was an attractive, young blond American woman who, as the story goes, overdosed in Herat, was found there wandering with little on. She was reportedly abused by men.. Their attitude was—well she dressed that way so was inviting it and besides, she was crazy, so what difference would it make, and most of all she was a foreigner, no family member near, no male to stand up and fight for her.

Someone got involved and got her to Kabul, where she escaped, was seen on the streets. Eventually the U.S. authorities stepped in and got her back to the United States.

Yes, some came for the drugs. You could smell hashish smoke walking on or near Chicken Street, the name given to a world traveler area in Shahre Naw, where there were flophouses, handicraft and rug stores, a range of restaurants, and super bakeries. These were run by former servants to USAID households. They were taught how to bake and were encouraged to go into business. Apple and fruit turnovers, super good brownies, baklava—many of the ingredients were organic, and they tasted wonderful.

Food stores and stalls, piled high with fruits. Huge pyramids of various citrus, especially in the winter—great for the constant cold, often bought by the seer, about sixteen pounds. Kebabs were everywhere, from smoky street stalls to quiet restaurants, as were pilaus—mounds of flavored rice with meat inside.

And of course, pots of black tea usually heated by huge antique Russian samovars. But in the afternoon, green tea was preferred: more appropriate to the afternoon, I was told.

Tea drinking was a ritual of hospitality. Life was simple, but people took pleasure and elegance in doing certain things with great style. Teas houses, *chai khanahs*, were everywhere. They ranged from bleak cement rooms with bare tables and chairs with echoing, blaring music to quieted adobe rooms to rooms with carpeted raised platforms, called *sofas* (our word comes from this). Sometimes simple wood platforms two or so feet off the floor, sometimes intricate wood platforms with railings on three sides, and in the north they were sometimes up a ladder into the low branches of a tree. Sometimes they were rectangular packed-mud platforms, sometimes centered in a sunken bed of flowers or under a tree.

Shoes would be removed and one sat on the usual red Turkoman rugs. The cylindrical polished brass Russian samovars often had czarist stamps. They heated the water, which was then poured into a pot with tea.

This was served to you along with handle-less cups and perhaps a small empty bowl. The ritual varied, but the host, or you, would take a cup and pour a little hot tea in it. You then swished it around and poured it out into the bowl, turning the cup as you did so that you further cleaned the rim. You would also pour tea from the pot over the outside rim of the cup as you held and turned it. Sometimes a little tea was used to warm up the cup and then poured into the bowl, or if outdoors, onto the ground. Some favored pouring the tea on the rugs on the floor as it enriched the color to deeper shades of red. The liquid quickly evaporated.

Hard sugar from sugar beets or regular sugar was served. In some cases, people would fill your cup about halfway with sugar, to which the tea was added. You drank this and then more tea was added, but no more sugar, so that you were gradually led from a very sweet cup to bitter. This flavored one's mood, and the mood of the conversation. Then the process was repeated. Sometimes hard candy was offered and one drank the tea through the candy in one's mouth. Putting a shell of cardamom in the tea was a sign of extra welcome.

Once several of us went to Jalalabad, a dusty, sprawled out-town in a large semitropical valley, full of Buddhist sites with the snow-capped mountains of Nuristan to the north, the White Mountains and Tora Bora to the south. It was en route from Kabul to the Khyber Pass, which led to Peshawar, Pakistan, and the rest of the subcontinent. We were driven to a village north of the town called Shewa. Here craftsmen made wooden bowls, sugar bowls with lids, with a small hole in the top through which one blew if the lid was stuck. These items were lacquered with a kind of wax, in mostly dark red hues. What struck me were the motifs and eight-spoked wheels, stylized triangular forms like a Buddhist stupa, clearly carried down from when this area was part of the great Gandha-ran Buddhist culture. The eight-spoked wheel is a clear Buddhist symbol.

As we shopped, we were invited to drink tea. Previously we had been cautioned that this area was outside of town—was in Pash-tun country and that there was little government, but strong tribal codes. We were told to be very respectful of local codes and behavior or we would be in trouble.

All this was very true, but as was the case in Afghanistan, the opposite, or a form of it, was also true at the same time. Many Afghans, even educated Kabulis, knew little of their country outside their city or original family area. They were often more scared or wary of different places than we were.

The town consisted of shop stalls on both sides of the road with adobe homes behind. Being very new to the country, we were unsure of our behavior. There was the formalness that was often present that could be a sign of respect, or—being naive as we were—it could be one of coldness.

We were poured and offered tea, and as we raised our cups we became aware of a lovely peculiar scent. No one was there to explain and for a few moments we were confused and very insecure. We didn't know what we were being offered—tea didn't smell like this. Was it bad water?—in which case we'd get very ill. And if we refused to drink that would be an insult, and that could lead to loss of face and who knew what. Then an Afghan said, "*Hell, hell, hell o chai.*" Then a translator came, laughed and explained that hell was the spice cardamom—which added to tea was a special gesture of welcome.

Eventually we all laughed, especially the Afghans.

## ᜂ 65 ᜂ

# Trip to the Khanagah

Nur Agha didn't have a car, but one day he told me he had just bought one. He was thrilled, he could now drive all over and do things he had wanted to. He said it was about power, about being freer. Then he invited me to go with him to a *khanagah* in the desert south of Kabul near Ghazni.

A *khanagah* is a building or a complex of buildings. Sometimes they were a very simple arrangement, but others were grand structures, such as in the ancient cities of Central Asia. Constructs of great beauty, large, beautifully proportioned inside and out, encrusted with tile on the inside and out.

Some, as in Bukhara, were part of a larger complex containing a mosque and a religious school that opened out onto a courtyard, some with stepped pools of water shaded by ancient trees. But unlike the open courtyards of the Persian-styled mosques, these khanagahs in a colder climate were roofed, often domed. They were for the use of Sufis and dervishes. A Sufi could be anyone who pursued deeper understanding and had a teacher. A dervish was someone who did this full-time. One used various exercises, zikrs, to expand one's consciousness, depending on the order one belonged to. And you joined an order based on your own personality structure and what helped you expand. Some, like the Mevlevi, danced or whirled, the "Whirling Dervishes." Others chanted; some, like the Chishti, played music; others did calligraphy or architecture or landscaping or whatever helped.

And some were more radical and did whatever would upset the social norms, whatever would cause people shock so that perhaps they might snap out of the ways they normally viewed the world and see it better, perhaps see it clearer for the first time.

If a community was ultraconservative and forbade music or dance, these more radical dervishes would come to the community play and sing and dance, or drink wine, or go naked. A rich member might go around dressed as a beggar or a beggar as a rich man just to shake up the social order, to get people to wake up and question whether they were really living or just blindly following traditional ways and norms. Some teachers would ask a disciple to do what was difficult for them. An active person might be asked just to do nothing, to waste time. A quiet person might be asked to talk and talk. Different steps led to different stages of awareness, and all these steps were just exercises. But one had to have a teacher; otherwise, one just followed one's self and went in circles. One needed someone from outside one's normal world. Someone who had the perspective to see you in "your world." A mirror.

I had told Nur Agha about observing zikrs, and about my curiosity. Now Nur Agha was eager for me to come to one. He said the ones I had seen in various places were his people, his Order, and that I would find it very interesting. I could bring a camera, shoot pictures, bring a movie camera, and bring a tape recorder. I could bring anything I wanted to and could document what went on there as people reached ecstatic states. I had permission to do whatever.

I was excited by his eagerness that I go. I had not met anyone who had gone to such a khanagah. Yes, dervishes, Sufis, doing zikr, their special exercises, I had witnessed. But going to a remote place in the open desert, this was something else; this would be

a wonderful adventure. And since I would be going under his invitation, I would not just be sitting as unobtrusively as possible
watching it all. This time I would be free to document it and be
more than welcomed. Of course this freedom had some very strong
limitations. Because I would be going with him, anything—everything—I did would reflect back on him. I'd have to be super obser-
vant and careful not to offend or show disrespect. I would have to
try to be worthy of his invitation. As we spoke about the logistics,
my initial wave of excitement receded and thoughts of problems
arose. I always found that having to be hyper-vigilant to what was
going on was exhausting. Then he set down his one precondition.
Yes, I could do anything I wanted, but at some point I had to join
them in doing these exercises. I was thrilled at this, I had wanted to
be in a zikr since the first time I saw dervishes in the Great Mosque
of Herat. I too could be in the circle of people chanting, all trying to
expand. And my mind, or whatever part of me it was, could go off
to other places to reach out to new experiences. I was drawn to this
and wondered what it would be like.

I recalled what I had seen: circles of people chanting slowly first
then faster and faster than eventually slow again. Standing they repeated *Allah Hoo*, The God that Is. They bowed on *Hoo* and then
went upright again on the name *Allah*. Up and down. Clearly they
were hyperventilating. Gradually the circle seemed to be just a single mass upright then bowed in half to the center, turbans flying
off, long hair flying. All the while, another person stood aside and
sang—a song that felt like a bird soaring above this heaving mass.
And one person stood in the center and moved to each person, facing each in turn. It seemed that he was checking each person individually to see that they were in sync with the others that they did
not go off by themselves that they were OK. I thought about this
and thought that Nur Agha might be the person in the middle. I
also recalled how passionate the people were. They were not just

chanting. Although in unison, they were inhaling air and exhaling words with such vehemence it was clear that they were almost desperately trying to reach out and touch something beyond, or that the other side was pulling them towards this other place. So instead of a calm meditation detachment, they were occupying, filling their bodies and minds with actions and words so that another part of themselves could go, could travel further, could leave the normal confines of their living and try to touch the God. It was a very strong, active kind of meditation.

It would be wonderful to participate in such a journey. But slowly an uneasiness crept over me. These people were all from one basic culture, religion, place. I was from outside—a different culture, religion, mind. So I asked him: When the people do zikr, they go to other places, right? "Bali, yes." The man in the center helps them stay together, right? "Bali." They go away, but he helps them came back, right? If there is a problem, he knows where to bring them back to, right? "Bali." But I am not like them. "Bali, *roast*. Yes, true." If there is a problem or something is off when it all gets very intense, do you know, do the others know where to bring me back to? He paused for a long time and looked at me. "That's a deep question. We will have to talk about this . . . "

I should add that the zikrs I saw there were much different from the ones I have visited in this country. Here it always seemed "nice and loving" somehow, and there, well, just like the poetry of Rumi, as they read it—it tears one's heart open. But in English translations it usually just sounds sincere and nice.

## ๑ 66 ๑

# A Tourist and a Story

One day I met a man, an American tourist who stood out, I guess because of his seriousness. We talked over tea and gradually he disclosed his reasons for being there.

This American said he was a Wall Street man who was very interested in Gurdjieff, Ouspensky, and Blavatsky—people from the turn of the twentieth century who traveled in Asia and set up esoteric schools of philosophy. He explained that he wanted to go to the secret lost monastery in Nuristan—where Gurdjieff studied. Asking people about a secret community in the Hindu Kush seemed odd, I said. Yes, but what other way could he learn its whereabouts, he asked. That evening I was supposed to go to an Afghan friend's home for dinner and told him perhaps my friend could help. I called and asked if I could bring him, and true to Afghan hospitality, we went. After the usual greetings and talk, we sat down to a wonderful meal, and the stock broker explained his quest. Agha said he had never heard of such a place, but in Afghanistan, who knew? He then told us some stories, one of which is . . . .

My friend's family was part of the royal clan, Mohammadzai, and in the 1700s and early 1800s, they warred with other clans for control. At one point, an ancestor of his had to flee the country. He went to Mashad, a large city in eastern Iran near the border, with a colossally wealthy Shiite shrine complex, dedicated to Imam Reza. Domes and minarets were covered with dazzling mosaics; some were gold plated. This shrine had vast endowments and, though unknown to most of the world, it is a major center of concentrated wealth. He and his party were safe there.

One night there was a knock on the door. In those days, this was not that usual. Night, even in cities, was a time to stay within heavy barred wooden doors. The mazes of narrow alleys were dark and deserted. At times, cries of night watchmen broke the silence. At the door a man with a lantern explained that he wanted Agha's ancestor to come with him in a carriage. The man assured him that he would be safe, but that a very important person wanted to meet with him and that this had to be done quietly and discreetly, and he was to be blindfolded. The man stressed that it was very important.

Intrigued, but extremely wary, he finally agreed, left his home, and followed the man down the alleys to a wider road where a black carriage with covered windows waited. He was blindfolded, entered the carriage, and was driven for a long time, turning right and left. He had no idea of where or how far he had gone. Finally the carriage stopped, the door opened, and he was led hand in hand into a building. Then led further in, room after room it seemed. The blindfold was removed and his eyes adjusted to the lights within a richly furnished Persian room, richly carpeted, with painted walls and a vaulted ceiling. There was a very peculiar feeling in the room. There were people there, but no great person yet. And the servants were not servants, yet very respectful and acted as if someone of great importance was there. On the far side was a curtain, and he was told to go through it. He parted the curtain and saw another room with what seemed like a large crib-like bed with high sides intricately decorated. A man's voice said, "Come here." He approached, and in the bed saw what appeared to be a large clothed baby with an old man's face and a long white beard. Shocked, he was told by the man not to be fearful. The man explained that he was pleased that he had come, and that he had nothing to fear. The old man spoke with great authority and explained that he was "Bab," which means gate. (But this name has layers of possible interpretation. It is even the name of a founder of the Baha'i religion). Agha's ancestor was told that he was allowed to tell others this, and no more. Then the old man spoke of his future and other topics and then told him to leave. He went to the other side of the curtain, where he was again blindfolded, led to the carriage, and driven again for hours until he at last returned home.

The American kept asking people about the secret community and eventually returned home. Years later I saw the movie *Meetings with Remarkable Men*, by Peter Brook, partly filmed in the country. The lost monastery scenes in it seemed very unconnected to

Afghanistan, but then who knew for certain . . . .

They say if you ask you will find. Yet, had I asked to meet Nur and other remarkable people I met there, I don't think it would have happened, nor would friendships have blossomed.

## ৬ 67 ৩

# The Gift of Joy-e Namaz

During my last days in country I sorted through my things, deciding what I should ship back to the States and what to give away and to whom. I gave Nur Agha a pile of English-language books and a much bigger collection of music tapes. Because he was a real Sufi, he really loved music. Some he knew of—Arabic tapes of Um Kalthum and Fairuz, but most were Western classical and American folk and rock. He was very curious about these as a way of understanding Western young people. Why were such large numbers passing through his country to India? He also said he liked Janis

Joplin, and the Beatles, though he didn't understand all the English lyrics.

One day I came over and he greeted me in the garden. He said he had something he wanted to show me inside the house. We went into his sitting room–bedroom, where we usually met in cold weather. If it was warm, or sunny, we would sit outside in the sun; this was the usual custom in the country. As soon as we went in, my eyes darted to the left, to the floor. There was something new there. He pointed to it and said, "Look, what do you think?"

It was a *joy-e namaz*, a "place to pray"—a prayer carpet. It was a simple weave, not finely knotted but not too coarse, wool pile on wool warp and weft. It was the usual size for one person, but it was otherwise unusual. It was not the typical subdued dark red Turkoman tones or dark-hued Baluch. It had a touch of the ever-present red, but there was a lot of dark tan, actually camel hair. And the design was very bold, but it was balanced. The central field was flanked by columns, but they were striped diagonally red and dark tan. It exuded brightness and it was a happy rug, it cheered you when you looked at it.

I was a student of rugs and spent many hours, looking, touching, smelling, learning. Some how the world seems to ignore the fact that the ancient art of weaving rugs is one of the glories of the world of women. It is mostly women who prepare, design and weave the rugs. It is surprising that museums, universities, authors do not educate people about this very prominent accomplishment of women. In these lands women are kept in the background and thus do not proclaim their work but one would think that world institutions would recognize this great contribution to world culture. Beyond the tribal divisions and their subdivisions, and designs, and old versus new, and discussions of natural dyes versus artificial dyes, and the various weaves and knots, I found that rugs struck me as either "happy rugs" or "not happy rugs." The happy, or joyous, pieces were not common. They had a delight in them, a very personal reflection of the weaver. Sometimes it was the colors, or the original touches in the design or in the weave. It usually was not anything specific that marked them as different, but the difference was unmistakable.

Some were pieces made for one's own family, or as part of a dowry, or were specially made for a person or occasion. Most rugs had a flatter feeling to them. They were just made, usually as a source of income. They might be of a much higher technical quality, the design might be exquisite and require great professional skill, but they were rugs; wonderful, but not happy. I found this all true for rugs from other countries too, from Turkish to exquisite Iranian pieces to the hand woven, virtual slave factory rugs of

Pakistan and India. Like a painting or a sculpture, rugs reflect the mind and soul of the weaver, the artist. There was one big difference, though: in the fine arts, you have to be gifted to produce good art. You could show what you were born with and develop skill in. But in traditional crafts, many people did them, and through repetition and training one could develop great skill and could express one's soul. In a way, more people had an opportunity to make art.

I admired the rug. Nur Agha was pleased. Then he picked it up and put it to the side. Underneath was another rug. I was shocked. "Oh . . . oh . . ." I had never seen such a design in a rug. Nur Agha was highly amused by my reaction.

It was another, a second prayer rug, but totally different from any I had ever come across. It was roughly the same size, but the wide border was white, gleaming white. You never saw this in an Afghan rug. Turkoman rugs were shades of red. Baluch were dark: brown, red, or bluish. Both had touches of white, but I had never seen so much in a single piece. Later there was a kind of rug that appeared on the market, Taimani, from the Herat area that used a lot of white, but they were not like this one.

The white border had a vine of dark flowers and leaves surrounding the central field. Inside this border the central rectangle was of camel hair. Three little domes at the top pointed the way to pray. There were a few white stars. But below this was the center of the design. It seemed to explode out from the tannish-brown field.

A large Greek cross design, made of four triangles, dominated the field. It was composed of a grid of small black and white squares. To the left and right of this were odd, jagged red lines, like crazy parentheses that framed the center. It was a wild and happy rug. It excited me. Nur Agha looked at me and said, "They are for you, take both of them."

I was shocked. I said, "They are prayer rugs. Where did they come from?"

He said they were gifts from the Baluchi people who were set-tling at Farah. They were made for him in thanks for representing them to the king and for the successful negotiations for the land. The people were very happy and excited by the prospect of starting new lives. They made these "happy" rugs for him. He was pleased with the gifts and now, seeing that I was leaving, wanted me to have them.

"I can't take them."

"No," he said, "Please, from me to you. Take both!"

"No, then you will not have a rug."

"No problem. They said they will make more rugs if I need them."

I had immediately fallen greatly in love with these rugs. They struck me by their uniqueness more than any other rugs I had ever seen. Yes, I wanted them, but I felt it was too generous a gift. It was too much. I said so, and Nur Agha and I argued about it. But I was firm. Then we argued about it some more. Finally I said, "You have been a wonderful friend and have taught me so much. That is enough." Nur just looked at me.

I left the country. It was winter and too cold and rough for the overland trip to Europe and a cheap flight home from there. So I went to India, where it was much warmer. Besides the northern Mughal sites, I also explored the south, Tamil Nadu and its fantas-tic temple cities. Then I went to Sri Lanka with all its lushness and problems. Both countries are shocking contrasts to Central Asia. In fact I was ill in Sri Lanka, and the doctor said it was mostly due to the body's acclimatizing to sea level tropical from high altitude desert. I had wonderful adventures with friends and then had to head back, through Kabul to Europe.

It was March in Afghanistan, and Nur Agha was not in Kabul, but in Jalalabad. I went to visit him there on his farm. It was spring, their Nauroz, New Year time. Everything was exploding into green. And the mountains gleamed with snow and ice. We were happy to see each other, and after exchanging greetings, he said, "Now you are going to take the rug, aren't you?" He stared, I laughed. All during the trip, my mind kept returning to that rug. I couldn't get it out of my head. Even though I had refused it as a gift, I still wanted it. And now back with Nur Agha, he read my mind and was offering me the gift of the rug again. I was surprised and said, "Bali, yes," eagerly. He laughed and said, "Good!"

As the rug was in his room in Kabul and he had to stay in Jalalabad, to direct the spring planting, he said he would send a servant to his home to notify his family that I would be coming to pick up the rug. He'd be up in a few days. It was late afternoon when I got to his house a few days later to pick up the rug. I rolled it up and carried it to the home of friends I was staying with. On the way there a policeman stopped me and asked what I was doing with a rug. I explained that I was going home, that I worked here, etc. He was upset but finally allowed me to go on. Later I learned that there was a law: it was illegal to carry rugs at night. It was assumed that you did your business during the daylight hours and that carrying a rug at night meant that you had stolen it. This was new to me. I was glad to reach my friends' house—it was warm and there would, as always, be a good dinner. They were curious about the rug so I unrolled it and draped it over the back of a rope chair. The electricity in their house was weak, so the light was dim. We sat in the floor looking at it and talking.

Suddenly, "Do you see what I see?"

"No, what?"

"Look, there in the border?"

"Where? Oh, yeah? Oh, no! Strange . . . "

I think we first noticed it in the white border area. The stylized flowers and vine and leaves now took on the appearance of eyes, then faces, and they were not smiling. There were eyes and faces everywhere, dark eyes in white, white eyes in brown. The flower pots and flower designs changed into angry faces, with threatening mouths. It was very unsettling. The nice happy rug seemed to have a life of its own, and what we saw were not nice, happy faces.

I had not expected this. This was a prayer rug! Why should it have faces in it? Were we imaging things? No, we checked and double-checked, moved it around. We all saw the same things. What was hidden in bright light became visible in the darkness, the opposite of normal logical investigation. This was all so unsettling that we rolled up the carpet.

When Nur Agha came back to town, I asked him what was going on. What did the symbols mean, why were there faces? He laughed and laughed. His explanation went like this. In the big cross design, the black and white are Sufi colors. It points to the four directions, north, south, east, west, and to eight, to sixteen. In the center is a rose, another Sufi concept. It is like when you throw a stone in water, the ripples go out to the four directions, north, south, . . . and the eight, northeast, southeast, . . . and the sixteen, north by northwest, and so on.

So what you do, any action you take, affects things, events, and people around you. The strange irregular parenthesis design framing the cross signifies that just as ripples go out and affect others and events, so then the effect of your actions came back to you, but not in the ways you expected. A similar idea is behind the faces. The flowers, the flower pots, what looks like what we take as beautiful, or as signs of love, may actually be the opposite, and much more. What we accept at one level may not be true at another level. What looks beautiful maybe ugly or even evil. We must be careful in life, not be controlled by our family, society, or culture. We must always look deeper, for what lies below or behind—for it is always there. But to do this, we must learn how to look deeper—to see.

I was reassured by his explanation and my unease over having a rug with monster faces hidden in it vanished. It was a teaching device, a reminder to always try to be aware of deeper levels of things. It was a microcosm of the whole culture and country. If you thought you understood it, you did not. What you saw was not necessarily what was there.

## ഌ 68 ‍ഌ

# We Are . . . A Rebab

As I was leaving the country, the plan was that a friend would volunteer to continue tutoring Nur Agha with his English. As it was winter, we went out to Jalalabad to make the introductions. The new teacher and Nur seemed to get along very well. Over tea we talked about many things.

Then he asked Nur Agha why he had never tried to convert me to Islam. Most Afghans respected your religion and did not push the point. In fact they sometimes grew suspicious of people very interested in their religion. In past historical experiences it had been tainted with espionage.

I always respected Nur Agha's beliefs, and he mine. But given the Islamic injunction to spread the faith by . . . . After all, the Western crusades were basically reactions to the Islamic crusades, jihad, which had conquered the non-Islamic lands of the Middle East, North Africa, Iran, and on and on. Afghans sometimes told stories about how they had resisted these invasions. The Hindu Ratbel-shahani kings of Kabul had even sent horses out to the Arabs when they were lacking so that the fight would be more sportsman-like. A fallen elephant in a city gate made it possible for the invaders to enter. The valley of Bamiyan supposedly reverted between Buddhist and Islamic beliefs eight or more times. Every time the Muslim armies would withdraw, the people would go back to their Buddhist ways. Finally, faced with annihilation by the Arabs if they did this again, they did not revert.

Very conservative Muslims would be upset with his answer. For them Islam is The religion, Jewish people and Christians are to be treated as a lower level as people with a "Book", but Hindus or Buddhists are not .

Nur Agha was quiet for a bit and said, "It is like this. You have a rebab"—the classical stringed instrument, deep and indented like a violin, with plucked strings and many sympathetic ones that vibrate when the others are hit, a rich, haunting sound. "Well," he said, "the different religions are like the strings on the rebab. The Muslims are like ting, ting, ting, the Christians are like tang, tang, tang, the Jewish people, pling, pling, pling, the Hindus plunk, plunk, plunk, the Buddhists . . . . Separate, each string is just sound, but together they make MUSIC, MUSIC, MUSIC to God!"—smiling, his arms waving in the air as if to music. His eyes large with delight and joy!

# In Thanksgiving

First there is starkness. So many countries and movements have sought to control and sway the country. Afghan elites have profited. The Everyday People have survived. The population has exploded, water decreases, deforestation, ecological degradation, overgrazing, poverty and drugs increase. Yet it holds minerals and oil and is in a pivotal geographic location. Currently the countries of the world say "we are out of Afghanistan", the problem is over. But closing one's eyes never solves a problem. The Taliban are teaching the young to see the world through their eyes. They have their age old world agenda. So perhaps soon the world will see large numbers of rigidly indoctrinated young men eager to spread their message. Women are suffering the most severe repression. The world does not agree with the Taliban. The larger Islamic World does not agree with the Taliban. Yet there is no movement. The country was massively armed and the men knew what would happen if the Taliban took control. Yet there was little resistance. Will the women arise? At this time nations say "we are out!" But they seem willfully blind to what is happening and to what will come out of this area.

The words Thank you are not enough to say to the wondrous ordinary people of Afghanistan who taught and gave me so much in the times I lived with them. The grace and sensitivity and kindnesses they extended to me cannot be fully measured or conveyed. My life was changed and made all the richer by their sharing of their lives with me. Many was the time when they, often in the depth of poverty or pain, silenced my mind and stretched my understanding of life with their exquisite dignity and the power of their actions and kindness—the smile, and not the eyes of hunger, but the penetrating eyes of wisdom of a child gathering bits of garbage to recycle, scraps of food . . . They deserve so much better than their leaders, and the powerful families of their country, their neighbors, the outside influences, the world, have made for them.

To all the people in this book, and to those not mentioned, I owe so much, Thank You!

This book would not have come to be except for the great hearts of two individuals, both angels, A. C. and D. H. Thank you!

Also great thanks to the many who have helped in so many ways. You know who you are. THANK YOU!